Entrepreneur
MAGAZINE'S
POCKET GUIDES

BUY OR DISCARD
LEASE A CAR

Without Getting Taken for a Ride

Entrepreneur Press and
Jason R. Rich

Ep
Entrepreneur Press

Editorial Director: Jere L. Calmes
Cover Design: Beth Hansen-Winter
Editorial and Production Services: CWL Publishing Enterprises, Inc.,
Madison, WI, www.cwlpub.com

This publication is designed to provide accurate and authoritative information in regard to the subject matter covered. It is sold with the understanding that the publisher and author are not engaged in rendering legal, accounting or other professional services. If legal advice or other expert assistance is required, the services of a competent professional person should be sought.

ISBN   13: 978-1-59918-079-3
       10: 1 -59918-079-0

Library of Congress Cataloging-in-Publication Data
  Buy or lease a car without getting taken for a ride / by Entrepreneur Press and Jason R. Rich.
    p. cm.
  ISBN-13: 978-1-59918-079-3 (alk. paper)
  ISBN-10: 1-59918-079-0 (alk. paper)
  1. Automobiles--Purchasing—United States. 2. Automobile leasing and renting—United States. I. Rich, Jason. II. Entrepreneur Media, Inc.
  TL162.B879 2007
  629.222029'73—dc22

                                                    2007002749

12 11 10 09 08 07   10 9 8 7 6 5 4 3 2 1

Contents

Introduction

Whether you plan to spend just a few thousand dollars on a used car or you have the money and financial wherewithal to spend $20,000 to $50,000 or even more on your new dream car, purchasing or leasing a vehicle involves making a lot of important and potentially costly decisions. With so many new and used vehicle choices available from dozens of manufacturers, selecting the perfect car to meet your wants and needs can be a challenge.

Buy or Lease a Car Without Being Taken for a Ride will help you define your needs, set your budget (figure out how much you can afford), and educate you on how to find the very best deals available, regardless of whether you plan to buy or lease a new vehicle or a used vehicle. This book is loaded with information, helpful tips, and useful advice that will help you determine exactly how much you can afford when purchasing and financing or leasing your vehicle and help you narrow down your options to the one vehicle that suits you best.

You'll also learn how to use the Internet to find out about all of the newest vehicles on the market or to locate the exact year, make, and model of used vehicle you want, shop around for the best price, and handle many of the other important steps involved with buying or leasing a car. Some of the information within this book comes directly from a handful of carefully selected car experts who have impressive credentials and who will provide you with greater insight into the car buying and leasing process.

Throughout this book, the term *car* and *vehicle* are used somewhat interchangeably (for simplicity's sake). These terms refer to *any* car, SUV, minivan, station wagon, sports car, sedan, pickup truck, or other category of motor vehicle that you would consider driving.

Speaking of terms you'll need to know, in each chapter you'll encounter *Car Speak* boxes. Each defines important terminology in an easy-to-understand way. Each chapter is also filled with *Driving Smart* boxes that will focus your attention on useful information provided to quickly convey important points, help you avoid common mistakes and pitfalls, or teach you how to save money.

As you'll soon discover, the car-buying process involves several key steps. Your ability to negotiate and perform research will help you save money as you complete each of these steps. Whether it's negotiating the best price for a vehicle or finding the very best financing or lease deal you qualify for, by investing a little time doing the right research, you can also save money, plus reduce the confusion and frustration many people often associate with buying or leasing a new or used car.

This book is loaded with information intended to help put you in the driver's seat of the vehicle that's ideal for you, based on your driving habits, needs, personal taste, and budget. It also stresses the need for you to do research in order to arm yourself with timely, accurate, and detailed information you'll want and need *before* you ever step foot into a car dealership or begin test driving vehicles for sale by owners. The need to conduct your own research can not be emphasized enough! However, thanks to the Internet and the resources described within this book, the amount of time you'll need to invest doing essential research will be minimal.

Once you identify your wants and needs and determine your budget, you can use the Internet to help you select a vehicle from the hundreds of makes and models available and then narrow down your choices to just a handful of suitable possibilities. In a matter of minutes, you can learn all about specific vehicles—performance, standard features, options, safety rating, consumer satisfaction rating, reliability, price, resale value, and other important matters. If you're shopping for a used car, you can also learn all about a specific vehicle's history in a matter of minutes using the Internet. This information can help you avoid buying a vehicle that will be costly to maintain and repair.

From the Internet you can learn what a dealer pays for a specific make and model of vehicle, what the manufacturer's suggested retail price is, what rebates or incentives are currently being offered, and what people just like you have recently paid for a comparable vehicle in your area. This is all important information that'll help you negotiate your best price and avoid paying more than necessary.

Best of all, much of the research you'll want to perform you can do anytime from the comfort of your home or office or anywhere else a computer is connected to the Internet. This book will teach you how to make the most of your time and money, reduce the stress of buying or leasing a car, and then help you make intelligent financial decisions.

From this book, you'll learn about how to purchase car insurance and you'll discover why so many people are now considering a hybrid vehicle rather than a traditional gas- or diesel-powered vehicle. Like all of the books in the popular *Entrepreneur Magazine's Pocket Guide* series, this one is designed to be easy to read and understand, whether you consider yourself to be a knowledgeable car enthusiast or you don't know the difference between an automatic transmission and a rear window defroster. Thanks to the information in this book and the free resources and tools available on the Web, you don't need to be too technically savvy to soon be driving a reliable and safe vehicle that you'll truly enjoy.

Driving Smart

KNOW WHERE YOU STAND FINANCIALLY Understanding how your credit score and credit history impact your ability to obtain the best vehicle financing deals or your ability to lease a vehicle is essential. The basics involved with understanding your credit report and credit score are offered in Chapter 2. However, you may find it useful to read Entrepreneur Magazine's Pocket Guide, *Dirty Little Secrets: What the Credit Bureaus Won't Tell You*. This book will teach you how to improve your credit score and get the best rates on loans and credit. It's also a valuable resource if you've damaged your credit rating and credit score and need to repair them in order to qualify for better vehicle financing or lease deals without needing a co-signer.

To learn more about all of the books in Entrepreneur Magazine's Personal Finance Pocket Guide series or to share your thoughts or car-shopping experiences with the author, visit www.JasonRich.com or www.EntrepreneurPress.com.

The first step in buying or leasing a car is to carefully define your exact needs, driving habits, and the vehicle that you consider to be perfect for yourself, based on your personal tastes. Setting a budget for yourself is also important. This is what's covered in Chapter 1, so turn the page and keep reading!

Choosing Your Vehicle

WHAT'S IN THIS CHAPTER

- Defining your transportation needs
- Understanding your driving habits
- Considering the types of vehicles
- Determining your budget
- Selecting a vehicle make and model

There are many well-known car manufacturers out there—BMW, DaimlerChrysler, Ford, General Motors, Honda, Hyundai, Nissan, Toyota, and Volkswagen, to name just the largest. Each manufacturer offers a unique lineup of vehicles.

In choosing the right vehicle, you should take into account five key factors, as they relate directly to you:

1. **Budget**—How much you can afford.
2. **Driving Habits**—How you'll be using the vehicle, in what weather conditions, and in what type of terrain.
3. **Needs**—What type of vehicle best suits your needs, based on how much driving you'll be doing, who your passengers will be, and what you'll be transporting.
4. **Personal Taste**—Color, style, optional features, and comfort all fall into this category.
5. **Wants**—There's a big difference between *wants* and *needs*. Your wants include the image you want the vehicle to convey and the optional accessories.

Before you start visiting dealerships, reading car reviews, applying for car loans, and going on test-drives, the first step in choosing the perfect vehicle is to carefully define your wants and needs. The initial steps described in this chapter apply whether you're in the market for a new or used vehicle and whether you're going to buy or to lease. This chapter focuses on helping you narrow down your options and find a vehicle you can afford, that serves your needs, and that you'll be happy and proud to drive for the next several years.

Ultimately, the vehicle you select must be one you can afford. This is especially important if you'll be financing it. In addition to the down payment and the monthly payments, this chapter explores some of the other one-time and ongoing expenses you'll need to work into your budget before acquiring a vehicle.

Sure, buying or leasing a car can be a time-consuming, confusing, and stressful process—but it doesn't have to be! The more you know about what you want and need, what you can afford, and what's available, the easier you make this process. This book, along with the research you perform, will make buying or leasing a car much easier, save you money, and keep you from getting taken for a ride by the dealer or owner. Let's start by defining your automotive needs.

Defining Your Transportation Needs

What will you need the car for? Use the following checklist to help ascertain your specific needs. This will help you ultimately choose the make and model that's best suited for you, your passengers, and whatever you'll be transporting.

For example, if you'll regularly be transporting three to four adults in a work carpool or a significant amount of luggage or equipment, you'll need a larger vehicle, so you eliminate smaller vehicles, such as two-door coupes or sports cars.

What Will the Primary Uses of the Vehicle Be?

Knowing who and what you'll need to transport will help you determine the size of the vehicle you need, based on seating and stowage capacity. Using the following checklist for reference, think about the primary ways you'll be using your vehicle.

❏ Commuting a short distance to/from work (under 20 miles each way)
❏ Commuting a long distance to/from work (over 20 miles each way)
❏ Performing errands around town (minimal driving)
❏ Driving long distances (more than 50 to 100 miles at a time)
❏ As a primary, all-purpose vehicle (at least 1,250 miles per month/15,000 miles per year)
❏ Carrying small items, such as grocery bags
❏ Carrying medium-size items, such as luggage
❏ Carrying large and heavy items, such as furniture, camping equipment, sporting equipment, or large boxes
❏ Transporting one or more children under age six
❏ Transporting one or more children over age six
❏ Transporting an average of two adults at a time
❏ Transporting two to four adults at a time
❏ Transporting more than five people at a time
❏ Transporting a pet
❏ Towing a trailer, boat, or other large or heavy items
❏ Using a special rack to transport bicycles, skis, or other sporting equipment

Understanding Your Driving Habits

In addition to defining your transportation needs, it's important to understand your driving habits and the driving conditions for the vehicle. Again, this will help you further narrow down your choices when choosing a vehicle. If, for example, safety is important and you'll be driving on wet, snow-covered, or icy roads, a larger and heavier vehicle with an excellent safety record and four-wheel drive may be very important to you.

What Type of Conditions Will You Primarily Be Driving In?

Where you live and the climate will play a large role in your vehicle's performance. For example, driving a car year-round in New England, which experiences hot summers and icy, snowy, and cold winters, will put a lot more wear and tear on the vehicle than driving it year-round in Florida or in a dry and warm climate, such as in Arizona.

Driving Smart

A vehicle that will be driven often in wet, icy, or snowy conditions should be equipped with four-wheel drive (or at least a good front-wheel drive system) and an anti-lock braking system (ABS) and with all-weather or winter tires for added safety.

ANTI-LOCK BRAKING SYSTEM (ABS)—A computer-controlled braking system that monitors the speed of the wheels and senses if braking is causing any difference in wheel speed that indicates a wheel is seizing and, if so, pulses the brakes to prevent that problem so the driver can maintain steering control. **CAR SPEAK**

What type of road conditions will you be driving in? Again, knowing this information will help you narrow down your choices.

❑ Dry, clear roads, speeds under 55 mph
❑ Dry, clear roads, speeds over 55 mph
❑ Wet roads, speeds under 55 mph
❑ Wet roads, speeds over 55 mph
❑ Snowy/icy roads, speeds under 55 mph
❑ Snowy/icy roads, speeds over 55 mph
❑ High temperatures
❑ Extremely low temperatures (freezing)
❑ Paved roads
❑ Unpaved roads
❑ Heavy traffic, stop-and-go driving

How Much Driving Will You Be Doing Each Year?

Knowing approximately how much driving you'll be doing per year will help you decide whether it's better for you to buy or to lease. In addition, it will help you determine how important fuel economy is when choosing the make and model of vehicle.

If you'll be using your vehicle for work-related purposes and taking a tax deduction for vehicle usage, knowing how much driving you'll be doing will help you calculate costs as well as tax savings.

FUEL ECONOMY—The number of miles a vehicle gets per gallon. All vehicle manufacturers are required to show on the sticker the fuel economy of each model, as estimates from the U.S. Environmental Protection Agency for city driving, highway driving, and combined driving.

CAR SPEAK

Based on your current driving habits, how much mileage do you anticipate putting on the vehicle during each month?

❑ Under 1,250 miles per month (15,000 miles per year)
❑ Over 1,250 miles per month

Driving Smart

Most car leases allow up to 15,000 miles per year. Beyond that, you will be charged extra per mile—anywhere from 15 to 35 cents or more. This extra charge can significantly increase the cost of the lease. Thus, if you'll be leasing a vehicle (a topic covered in Chapter 6), you want to ensure you'll be driving less than the allowable mileage. If you'll be putting significant mileage on the vehicle each year, leasing may not be a cost-effective option for you.

Driving Smart

Based on the amount of driving you'll be doing and the average gas mileage of the vehicle, you can calculate your approximate fuel costs using a fuel savings calculator, like the one found on the Honda Web site (*www.automobiles.honda.com/tools/calculators/mileage_calculator.asp*) . Enter the average price of gas per gallon, the number of miles you typically drive per day or month or year, and the average highway mileage your vehicle offers and this calculator will show how much you'll spend on gas for five years and ten years. There's a similar calculator on the www.fuele-conomy.gov Web site (*www.fueleconomy.gov/feg/savemoney.shtml*). Enter the average price of gas per gallon, the average miles per gallon, and the number of miles you drive per year to calculate the total fuel cost for the time you'll be driving your vehicle.

Considering the Types of Vehicles

There are many words used to describe vehicles based on their body style, size, seating capacity, and type. The following are basic descriptions of popular vehicle types (sometimes referred to as their *EPA class*). Virtually all cars on the market should fit into one of the following categories:

Driving Smart

As a general rule, smaller cars (such as two-door coupes, convertibles, and sports cars) tend to be more fuel-efficient, but seating and stowage capacity are less. Small cars typically do not offer four-wheel drive. Smaller cars tend to be less rugged than full-size vehicles, SUVs, or minivans.

- **Two-Door Coupe**—This is a compact vehicle, with two doors and typically comfortable seating for two adults. Some vehicles offer a small backseat, but legroom is often limited. Stowage space is also limited. The 2007 Honda Accord Coupe LX five-speed MT is an example of a popular, mid-priced two-door coupe.

- **Four-Door Sedan**—This is a full-size vehicle with co able seating for four to five adults, ample trunk stowage space, and plenty of legroom. These cars are designed for comfort and typically offer a wide range of features, like a high-end sound system, a global positioning system (GPS), cruise control, electric windows and locks, power seats, superior climate control, and cup holders. The 2006 Chrysler Sebring Sedan Base is an example of a relatively low-priced, but nicely equipped four-door sedan. Another example would be the 2006 Ford Five Hundred.

- **Convertible/Sports Car**—This is typically a small car. A convertible has a removable or retractable roof and is more suitable for driving in a warm climate. A sports car has a sleek, aerodynamic design and is typically designed for performance and speed, although it's often for status as much as for performance. Most convertibles and sports cars offer ample seating for two adults. Some have a small backseat area with limited legroom and stowage space. The 2006 BMW Z4 Roadster 3.0si is an example of a convertible sports car.

- **Full-Size Car**—This is a car that can seat four or five adults comfortably and has ample trunk stowage space and plenty of legroom. A full-size vehicle is often a top choice as a family vehicle, since it also has many safety features. This is often a four-door sedan. The 2007 Volvo S60 is an example of a mid-priced, full-size, four-door sedan. The Chevrolet Impala is another example.

- **Hybrid**—This is any vehicle that uses two or more sources of power, typically an electric motor with batteries and a gas- or diesel-powered engine. These are known as hybrid electric vehicles (HEVs) and, as of 2007, they're the most common hybrids. Hybrid vehicles (also called "green cars") are typically small to mid-size vehicles (although there are also hybrid SUVs) designed to be environmentally friendly. Hybrid cars use less gas because they take advantage of alternate fuel sources, such as natural gas, ethanol, or electricity. In some cases buying a hybrid also offers significant tax advantages. The 2007 Toyota Prius Touring is an example of a popular, mid-priced, mid-sized four-door hybrid vehicle. Chapter 11 focuses specifically on hybrids.

- **Luxury Car**—This is typically a full-size, mid- to high-priced vehicle that offers top-of-the-line features and options. Comfort, aesthetics, and luxury are the primary focus of the design. These vehicles tend to be status symbols. A high-end audio system, a GPS, leather seats, a sunroof, separate driver/front passenger climate controls, cup holders that heat or cool beverages, a rearview camera, and real wood trim are among the popular features in many luxury vehicles. You'll find luxury vehicles available from manufacturers like Mercedes-Benz, Bentley, Lexus, and Volvo, to name just a few.

- **Mid-Size Car**—This is a vehicle smaller than a full-size sedan, with comfort and features but slightly less stowage space. A typical mid-size car has either two or four doors, can hold four or five passengers, and has a small to-mid-size trunk (capable of holding one large or two small suitcases). The 2007 Chevrolet Monte Carlo LT is an example of a mid-priced, two-door, mid-size vehicle capable of holding five passengers.

- **Minivan/Cargo Van**—This is a large vehicle, capable of holding seven passengers with plenty of stowage space. Many of these vehicles offer fold-down or removable seats, allowing additional stowage space. Many mini-vans have three to five doors—two in the front, one or two sliding side doors, and a rear door (offering access to stowage space). The seven-passenger 2007 Honda Odyssey EX is an example of a mid-priced minivan designed for families.

- **Pick-Up Truck**—This is a vehicle with a front compart-ment that can hold two to six people (depending on the make and model) and an open cargo box. A pick-up truck is ideal for transporting large and heavy items and for towing. It can be driven on a wide range of ter-rains and in harsh weather conditions. One aspect to consider with pick-up trucks is payload capacity—how much weight the vehicle can carry. The popular Ford F-150 is a perfect example of a mid-priced, full-size, all-purpose pick-up truck.

- **Small/Compact Car**—This is usually a two-door coupe or a three-door hatchback capable of seating two to four adults. These cars tend to offer better gas mileage than mid- to full-size vehicles, but less stowage space. The 2007 VW Beetle is the perfect example of a two-door, mid-priced, compact vehicle.

- **Station Wagon/Five-Door**—This is a car with a passenger compartment that extends to the back, where there is a tailgate or a liftgate. A station wagon was a popular choice for a family car prior to the introduction of the SUV and the minivan. These vehicles tend to be larger and heavier, with more safety features and more stowage space. Many station wagons offer the comfort and features of a luxury sedan, but significantly more passenger and stowage space. The 2007 Volvo V70 is an example of a traditionally styled, five-door station wagon.

- **Sport Utility Vehicle (SUV)**—This is a mid-to-large-size vehicle with plenty of space, seating for five to seven people, and plenty of stowage space. These are a top choice among families, particularly in the suburbs, although their popularity has spread considerably. SUVs offer features designed to provide maximum comfort; of particular interest to families, many SUVs now come with a DVD video system in addition to a full-featured sound system and satellite radio receiver. These vehicles are designed for safety in virtually all weather conditions and typically offer real-time four-wheel drive or constant four-wheel drive. Due to their size and weight, unfortunately SUVs have lower fuel economy. An example of a mid-size SUV is the 2007 Honda Element. An example of a full-size SUV is the 2007 Hummer H3.

Driving Smart

Most popular manufacturers offer one or more models in each of these categories. For each model there's wide range of options and accessories, giving drivers many choices and the ability to truly customize their driving experience. Once you know what type of vehicle you need and your budget, narrowing down your options is much easier.

Determining Your Budget

One of the key factors in deciding which make and model of vehicle to buy or lease will be based on its *manufacturer's suggested retail price (MSRP)* and what you can afford. A vehicle's MSRP will give you a rough idea how much the car will cost, but you need to take into account a wide range of additional fees and expenses to determine whether or not you can afford a specific vehicle.

MANUFACTURER'S SUGGESTED RETAIL PRICE (MSRP)– *CAR SPEAK*
This is the price set by the manufacturer for the vehicle as it comes from the factory. The MSRP is typically *not* the price a consumer pays for the vehicle, however. When negotiating the price with the dealer, you'll want to consider the vehicle's *invoice price, base price, Monroney sticker price,* and *dealer sticker price*—all terms that are defined in Chapter 3. Rebates, incentives, and financing terms will also affect the price you'll pay.

Driving Smart

For the average person, car-related expenses should represent no more than 20 percent of gross monthly salary. If your take-home pay is $5,000 per month, for example, don't plan on spending more than $1,000 per month on your car payment *and* all car-related expenses (gas, insurance, parking, etc.). This general guideline works well, especially considering what you're spending for other monthly payments, such as rent or mortgage, basic living expenses, credit card bills, and loans.

If you're financing the vehicle (which is covered in Chapters 4, 5, and 6), you'll need to calculate the total price, with the down payment, monthly payment, interest rate, and financing terms.

Beyond the total cost of the vehicle, buying or leasing a car entails a variety of other one-time and ongoing expenses that you'll want to consider in advance. Calculating these costs will help you ensure that the vehicle you select remains within your budget. These are the fees and expenses you're apt to encounter.

Extended service contract or extended warranty (option)—*one-time or ongoing:* This expense is for additional, often costly coverage against certain types of problems with the vehicle after the manufacturer's warranty expires. Know exactly what is and not covered before purchasing this coverage.

Gas—*ongoing:* This expense depends on the prices and the amount of driving you'll be doing.

Insurance—*ongoing (monthly, semiannual, or annual):* Your monthly or annual premium will vary according to the amount of coverage, the deductible, your geographic area, your driving record, the type of vehicle, and the insurance company. (It's important to insure not only the vehicle but also the driver, passengers, and third parties. See Chapter 10.)

License, title, and registration—*annual:* The amounts of these fees vary. The dealer may charge you a small fee to handle this paperwork for you.

Maintenance costs—*ongoing:* The costs of keeping the vehicle in working condition include regular oil changes, routine maintenance, tire maintenance, and repairs. As part of your research, determine the average repair and maintenance costs for each make and model vehicle you consider.

Options and accessories—*one-time:* Among the options and accessories available for most vehicles are GPS navigation systems, high-end sound systems, DVD video systems, leather seats, and alarm systems.

Parking—*ongoing:* How much will it cost to park your vehicle at home and/or at work? Will you need to use parking meters, pay for hourly parking in a lot or a garage, or rent a monthly parking space?

Sales tax—*one-time:* The sales tax you'll pay if you purchase a vehicle. It can be added to the amount you finance.

Vehicle excise tax—*ongoing:* This is a local annual tax based on the value of the vehicle.

Delivery and prep charges—*one-time:* These are fees the dealership charges in order to cover the cost of transporting the vehicle from the factory and then preparing it for sale. These fees can often be negotiated down or eliminated.

Tolls and commuting expenses—*ongoing:* These are fees associated with driving your vehicle. If you use toll roads daily, these fees can add up and you should include them in your monthly budget.

> *CAR SPEAK* **VEHICLE EXCISE TAX**—This is a local annual tax based on the value of the vehicle, levied by the city or town where the vehicle is principally garaged. The tax rate and the calculation of the amount vary by region. Questions about your motor vehicle excise should be directed to your local Board of Assessors. For the first two or three years you own a new vehicle, this tax can be hundreds, perhaps thousands of dollars; you should include it in your budget and pay it in a timely manner to avoid penalties—more expenses.

Calculating the Cost of a Vehicle

Before committing to purchase or lease a vehicle, consider all of the costs, not just the negotiated price of the vehicle or your monthly loan payment. Many of these fees are in addition to and separate from your monthly payment. The following worksheet will help you calculate the one-time and ongoing costs of owning or leasing a vehicle.

Buy or Lease a Car Without Getting Taken for a Ride

Vehicle Cost Calculation Worksheets

Vehicle Financing Information	Amount
Negotiated Price (including all options and accessories and sales tax)	$
Amount to be Financed	$
Finance Rate (APR)	%
Finance Charge	$
Number of Monthly Payments (Length of Loan)	

One-Time or Annual Expenses	Amount
Down Payment	$
Tax, Title, and Registration Fees	$
Extended Services Contract	$
AAA Membership/Roadside Assistance	$
Vehicle Excise Tax	$
Delivery and Prep Charges	$
Total One-Time Expenses	**$**
Total Annual Expenses	**$**

Monthly (Ongoing) Expenses	Amount
Monthly Car Payment	$
Anticipated Monthly Fuel Expense (based on use and EPA mileage estimate)	$
Mileage (estimate)	
Insurance	$
Parking and Tolls	$
Maintenance (oil changes, tires, brake pads, windshield wiper blades, etc.)	$
Total Monthly/Ongoing Expenses	$

Selecting a Make and Model

There are ten criteria that are often used to choose a vehicle. Based on your personal situation, not all of these criteria may be important to you, but you should consider all of them. These criteria will help you decide what you want and need and then you can use them to quickly evaluate if a specific make and model meets those requirements. Listed here, in alphabetical order, are the ten common criteria used for selecting a vehicle:

1. **Body Style and Size**—This refers to the type of vehicle, ranging from a compact to a full-size SUV.

2. **Features and Options**—All vehicle manufacturers offer a wide range of built-in features, designed to provide comfort, versatility, and functionality. As you shop, note which features

are standard and which features are available for an extra charge. Then you can better compare models. For example, leather seats, a GPS navigation system, a satellite radio, an automatic transmission, and anti-lock brakes are standard on some vehicles, but optional (at a cost) for others.

3. **Fuel Economy**—Every vehicle being sold through a dealership is required to display EPA fuel mileage estimates for city and highway and the capacity of the fuel tank. Actual mileage will vary. This information will help you calculate fuel costs.

Driving Smart

To quickly research fuel efficiency ratings for vehicle make and models, visit *www.fueleconomy.gov*. You can download guides or compare vehicle models simultaneously online using this free service. This Web site is operated by the U.S. Environmental Protection Agency and the U.S. Department of Energy.

4. **Monthly Payment**—The purchase price of the vehicle is important, but once you've decided to finance or lease the vehicle, you may want to focus on the monthly payment, which is how much the vehicle would cost you every month throughout the life of the loan (typically three to five years) or the term of the lease.

5. **Purchase Price**—This is the amount you agree to pay for the car, complete with all of the features and options you select, plus sales tax and other charges. This price is different from

the vehicle's MSRP. The purchase price is typically calculated after you've negotiated with the dealer.

6. **Resale Value**—The moment you drive a new vehicle off the dealer's lot, it immediately drops in value and becomes a used car. Some vehicles retain their value better than others. If you plan on selling your vehicle at some point, how well it retains its value will be an important consideration. Many organizations publish guides that list resale values of cars by year, make, and model; the condition of the vehicle also plays a role in determining resale value.

7. **Safety Record**—This is information published by the car manufacturers as well as third-party organizations and the government. *Consumer Reports* and the National Highway Traffic Safety Administration (*www.nhtsa.dot.gov*) publish crash test and rollover ratings for every make and model of vehicle, as well as information about recalls. The Insurance Institute for Highway Safety (*www.highwaysafety.org*) is

Driving Smart

To quickly research crash test and rollover ratings for any vehicle (searchable by year, make, and model), visit *www.safercar.gov*, a Web site operated by the National Highway Traffic Safety Administration. You can also reach this organization by phone toll-free at (888) 327-4236 or (800) 424-9153 (TTY). The Center for Auto Safety (*www.autosafety.org*) is an independent, nonprofit organization that offers vehicle safety information. Don't rely on advertising or a salesperson at a dealership to provide you with accurate and up-to-date information.

another resource for learning about the safety record of specific vehicle makes and models.

8. **Service Record**—Some manufacturers have developed a strong reputation for reliable and well-built vehicles that require minimal maintenance. Third-party research is available that estimates how much you can expect to pay in maintenance and repairs for owning a specific make and model of vehicle. This research is based on national averages, but is a good indicator of the reliability of a vehicle make and model.

9. **Vehicle Make**—This is the manufacturer of the vehicle and its reputation. The reputation of each dealership also comes into play.

Driving Smart

J.D. Powers is an independent market research firm that annually publishes up-to-date consumer ratings for every vehicle make and model. You can access this information on the company's Web site at *www.jdpower.com/autos*. When you enter a make and model, you can access J.D. Powers manufacturing/design ratings in various categories, including overall quality, mechanical quality, body and interior quality, and features and accessories quality. The National Highway Traffic Safety Ratings are also offered, as well as specifications for each vehicle make and model.

10. **Warranty**—Every new vehicle (and almost every used vehicle, depending on how it's purchased) comes with a manufacturer's warranty. How long this warranty lasts and what's covered varies greatly by manufacturer and car

model. Warranties typically last for three to five years or for 30,000 to 100,000 miles, whichever comes first. The better the warranty coverage, the less you'll have to spend on repairs, at least during the warranty period. For an additional fee, you can typically purchase an extended warranty package, from either the manufacturer or the dealer.

Most consumers will use a combination of these ten criteria to narrow down their choices before visiting dealerships and taking test-drives. Of course, knowing your needs and driving habits will help you narrow down your options more quickly.

While this book offers detailed advice on how to find the ideal vehicle and then navigate through the often confusing buying or leasing process, it does not offer the latest information on specific car models. To obtain details about all of the latest car models offered by the popular manufacturers, you can purchase a printed guide, such as *Kelley Blue Book* (*www.kbb.com*), *Consumer Reports New Car Buying Guide* (*www.consumerreports. org/cro/cars/index.htm*), or *NADA Guides* (the National Automobile Dealers Association) (*www.nada.com*). You can also obtain this information online from one of the popular car-related web sites, including Edmunds.com (*www.edmunds.com*), Vehix.com (*www.vehix.com*), AOL Autos (autos.aol.com), or Yahoo! Autos (autos.yahoo.com).

The American Automobile Association (AAA) publishes useful information about new car models for its members. AAA can also help members locate reputable car dealerships, acquire auto financing, and assist with other aspects of the car-buying process. For details, visit *www.aaa.com* or call (800) 222-4357.

Yet another option is to visit the Web site or local dealerships for each of the car manufacturers that you're considering. If you visit a dealership, you can inspect and test-drive each vehicle and get answers to your questions from a salesperson. Reading car enthusiast magazines (available at newsstands) is another way to learn about specific makes and models of cars and to read detailed reviews about them. Chapter 4 provides information on buying a new car and choosing a dealership, while Chapter 6 focuses on working with a used car dealership.

Driving Smart

Chapter 8 provides information about using the Internet in buying a car and gives details about many of the popular car-related Web sites that make doing research and learning about specific makes and models of cars extremely fast and easy. Using these Web sites makes it easy to compare similar models from different manufacturers and narrow down your options according to your specific criteria, such as body type, features, safety ratings, warranty, consumer satisfaction ratings, resale value, and price.

Selecting Features and Options

After you've narrowed down your selection to a type of vehicle and maybe a manufacturer and even a specific model, focus on the options and accessories available. In addition to the features that come standard from the manufacturer, you'll discover a wide range of options available for an additional fee. Depending on which ones you choose, the price of the vehicle will rise, perhaps dramatically. Focus on what you need and what you'll use the most, based on your driving habits.

Popular Vehicle Manufacturers

You can use the following chart to locate local new car dealerships representing specific manufacturers or to learn about the latest vehicles. Many of these Web sites allow you to select options to configure vehicles online, obtain price quotes, and do extensive research on specific models. As you'll learn in Chapter 7, starting your car-buying or -leasing process online makes a lot of sense, will save you time, and can save you a fortune.

Car Manufacturers and Web Sites

Acura	www.acura.com
Aston Martin	www.astonmartin.com
Audi	www.audiusa.com
Bentley	www.bentleymotors.com
BMW	www.bmwusa.com
Buick	www.buick.com
Cadillac	www.cadillac.com
Chevrolet	www.chevrolet.com
Chrysler	www.chrysler.com
Dodge	www.dodge.com
Ferrari	www.ferrariworld.com

Ford	www.ford.com
GMC	www.gmc.com
Honda	automobiles.honda.com
Hummer	www.hummer.com
Hyundai	www.hyundaiusa.com
Infinity	www.infinity.com
Isuzu	www.isuzu.com
Jaguar	www.jaguarusa.com
Jeep	www.jeep.com
Kia	www.kia.com
Lamborghini	www.lamborghini.com
Land Rover	www.landrover.com
Lexus	www.lexus.com
Lincoln	www.lincoln.com
Lotus	www.lotuscars.com
Maserati	www.maserati.com
Maybach	www.maybachusa.com
Mazda	www.mazda.com
Mercedes-Benz	www.mbusa.com
Mercury	www.mercuryvehicles.com
Mini	www.miniusa.com
Mitsubishi	www.mitsubishicars.com
Nissan	www.nissanusa.com
Panoz	www.panoz.com
Pontiac	www.pontiac.com
Porsche	www.porsche.com/usa
Rolls-Royce	www.rolls-roycemotorcars.com

Saab	www.saabusa.com
Saturn	www.saturn.com
Scion	www.scion.com
Subaru	www.subaru.com
Suzuki	www.suzikiauto.com
Toyota	www.toyota.com
Volkswagen	www.vw.com
Volvo	www.volvo.com

Affording the Car You Want

If you plan to obtain a loan to purchase a new or used vehicle or you plan to lease a new vehicle, your credit history and credit score will play a tremendous role in your ability to obtain credit and acquire a loan at the lowest possible rate.

The next chapter focuses on understanding how your credit history and credit score impact your ability to obtain financing and it suggests ways to save money when choosing and acquiring any type of car loan, regardless of your credit history. If, however, you have below-average credit, you can expect to pay significantly higher fees and interest when financing. You may also find it difficult to lease a car if your credit score is below average.

Your Credit Score and Financing

WHAT'S IN THIS CHAPTER

- Understanding your credit history
- The importance of your credit rating and credit score
- Obtaining your credit report and credit score
- Five strategies for boosting your credit score
- Determine the interest rate and financing terms for which you qualify
- Vehicle financing options for people with bad credit

U nless you'll be paying for your vehicle with cash, you'll probably need to finance at least part of the cost. This means applying for and obtaining approval for a car loan, from the dealership's financing department, a bank or a credit union, or another lending source.

If you have a strong *credit rating* (*credit history*) and above-average *credit score*, obtaining approval for a car loan will be a fast and relatively effortless process. However, you will want to shop around for the very best deal in order to save money over the life of the loan on both fees and interest charges.

Driving Smart

If you're planning to finance your vehicle, in most situations you'll need to make a down payment of 10 to 20 percent, based on the negotiated price of the vehicle, so plan your finances accordingly. Dealerships often expect higher down payments from people with below-average credit.

CAR SPEAK **CREDIT RATING (CREDIT HISTORY)**—An educated estimate of a person's creditworthiness, a prediction of the likelihood that the person will pay a debt and the extent to which the lender is protected in the event of default. From a potential lender's standpoint, your credit rating indicates how likely you are to pay off your loan on time with interest. Your credit rating is calculated based on several factors, including your bill-paying history and the relationships you've maintained with past and current creditors and lenders.

CREDIT SCORE—A mathematical calculation of a person's creditworthiness, in which a credit reporting agency applies a complex formula to his or her current financial situation and credit history. A credit score will be between 300 and 850. The national average is about 675.

If your credit history is shaky and your credit score is below average, you will probably find it more difficult to get approved for an auto loan, especially if you're trying to finance a new car through a dealership. While almost anyone with a steady job can get approved for some type of auto loan (since there are some lenders out there willing to approve loans for people who are a high credit risk), someone with below-average credit will always pay significantly higher fees and interest for any loan. Over time, this dramatically increases how much you'll pay for the vehicle.

Paying too much in interest and fees over the life of a loan is one way you could wind up being upside-down on a loan if you attempt to sell your vehicle before you've paid off the loan totally. Being "upside-down" means owing more on the car (the loan amount outstanding) than the car is worth. Thus, to sell the vehicle, you'll need to pay out-of-pocket for the difference between the amount you receive for the car and the amount you still owe.

For example, suppose you owe $10,000 on your vehicle and still have three years left of monthly payments to pay off the loan, yet you want or need to sell the vehicle immediately. You do research and determine that your car is worth at best only $6,000 if you sell it privately (as opposed to using it as a trade-in to buy another car at a dealership). Thus, you would still owe $4,000 on your loan, even if you manage to sell the car for $6,000. When you sell your vehicle, you'll still need to come up with $4,000 in cash. This means you're upside-down on the loan, a bad position. Because you have to pay a high interest rate and high fees on your loan, less of your monthly payments goes toward the loan's principle and more goes toward interest charges and fees.

What Happens if You Don't Pay?

If you fail to make your monthly car payments in a timely manner, here's the scenario. The finance company will eventually repossess your vehicle. This means the car will be taken away from you and sold, generally at auction for below market value. The amount received for the vehicle will go toward what you still owe on your loan. Even after the vehicle is repossessed, you will still owe the money on the loan, as well as repossession and legal fees. Plus, the repossession will be a negative mark on your credit report for seven years and reduce your credit score significantly. With a repossession on your credit report, you will find it considerably more difficult to get approval for another auto loan or other forms of loans or credit.

Understanding Your Credit History

When you apply for auto financing, you will complete the application, which will request information, including your full name, your address, your phone number(s), the name of your employer, your income, and your Social Security number.

Then, one of the first things the dealership, bank, financial institution, or potential lender will do is obtain copies of your *credit reports* and *credit score* from all three *credit reporting agencies* (*credit bureaus*)—Equifax, Experian, and TransUnion.

Information displayed on your credit report and your credit score will play a tremendous role in the approval process with any potential lender. Your credit report lists information about you and your credit history, including your relationship with your current and past lenders and creditors. By looking at your credit report, a potential lender can determine if you have a positive history of paying your bills on time. Your credit history and the information that appears on your credit reports (which are compiled by the credit bureaus) determine your credit score, which is an indicator that potential lenders and creditors commonly use when making approval decisions for loans and credit.

At least 45 to 60 days before you start shopping for a new or used car, obtain copies of your credit reports and credit scores from each of the three credit bureaus. The process for doing this is described later in this chapter. If you review your credit reports and credit scores in advance, you can determine how much of a loan and what loan terms you'd potentially qualify for. Thus, you can further narrow down your options in terms of vehicle makes and models, based on what you can afford.

Each time you apply for a loan, credit card, or some type of financing, the potential lender will obtain copies of your

CAR SPEAK   **CREDIT REPORT**—This is a credit file disclosure compiled by one of the credit reporting agencies—Equifax, Experian, or TransUnion—that contains personal and financial information, including name, address, phone number, Social Security number, date of birth, past addresses, current and past employers, a listing of companies that have issued credit to that person (including credit cards, charge cards, car loans, mortgages, student loans, and home equity loans), and details about his or her credit history. Each of the major credit reporting agencies compiles a separate credit report for every individual. However, much of the information on the three reports should be the same or extremely similar. Information on your credit reports is updated monthly by your creditors and lenders. This information is based on how timely you pay your bills—not on your current income, the amount of money you currently have in your checking or savings account(s), or the value of your assets.

CREDIT REPORTING AGENCY (AKA CREDIT BUREAU)—Any of the three national bureaus—Equifax, Experian, and TransUnion—that maintain credit histories on virtually all Americans with any credit history and supply creditors and lenders with timely and reliable financial reports as requested. These agencies maintain vast databases that are updated regularly. Their purpose is to supply creditors with timely and reliable financial information about individual consumers. It's important to understand that a credit reporting agency does *not* decide whether an individual qualifies for credit or not. Credit reporting agencies simply collect information that is relevant to a person's credit history and habits and then provides that information (for a fee), in the form of a credit report, to creditors and lenders.

credit report and credit scores from one or more of the credit bureaus. This is referred to as "pulling credit reports." This is considered an "inquiry." The number of inquiries made about your credit is tracked by the credit bureaus and will be held against you. In fact, each time an inquiry is made and a potential creditor or lender accesses your credit report, your credit score will temporarily go down slightly.

When you're shopping for a mortgage or car loan, however, the credit bureaus allow you to have your credit reports pulled as many times as needed, by as many potential lenders as you wish, during a 30- to 45-day period (depending on the credit bureau). Thus, whether you have one inquiry or ten inquiries about possibly financing a vehicle during that period, it will count as only one inquiry in terms of the impact on your credit score. All of the inquiries, however, will appear on your credit report immediately. So, if you've shopped at six dealerships and you're currently visiting your seventh dealership, that dealership will know where you've already shopped and whether or not you were approved for financing through those dealerships if you completed loan applications at those places. The dealership's financing department or the

Driving Smart

Keep in mind that requesting copies of your own credit report and credit score does *not* damage your credit rating or lower your credit score.

Unless you're serious about purchasing a vehicle from a specific dealership, don't allow a dealership to pull your credit report and don't fill out a loan application, even if you're pressured to do so by the salesperson or finance manager.

financial institution can hold this information against you when making its decision on your application.

How Your Credit Score Is Calculated and What It Means

Your credit score is a three-digit number that is an indicator of your creditworthiness. In other words, it's a tool that helps creditors or lenders gauge the level of risk they would incur if they approved you for a loan or granted you credit.

Your credit report includes detailed information about your current credit, your payment history, and other data a creditor or lender can use to make intelligent decisions about whether or not to trust you with money. In the past, for a creditor to make this decision required a person with specialized training who would carefully analyze all of the information on someone's credit report manually and then make a determination about his or her creditworthiness. That was how things were done about two decades ago. Today, thanks to computers, the process is far more automated and decisions can be made in seconds, not hours or days, thanks to credit scoring.

Using only information from your credit report, a complex mathematical algorithm is used to calculate a credit score based on a variety of criteria, each of which is weighted differently. The result is a number between 300 and 850 that represents how much of a credit risk you represent.

Someone with a history of being an extremely high credit risk would have a credit score in the 300s or 400s, while someone who is considered a good credit risk would have a score in the mid 600s to low 700s. Someone with a credit score in the mid- to high 700s or in the 800s is considered an excellent credit risk. These are the people who get the lowest interest rates, for example, when applying for loans and credit cards.

It's important to remember that different lenders and creditors give different weight to these scores. When making their decision to approve a loan or credit, here's how lenders and creditors generally perceive credit scores and *FICO® scores*:

Excellent	Above 750
Very Good	720 to 750
Acceptable (Average)	660 to 720
Uncertain	620 to 660
High Risk	Below 620

Driving Smart

FICO® SCORE—Your credit score is sometimes called your *FICO® score*. FICO® is a registered trademark of Fair Isaac Corporation (NYSE:FIC), the pioneer of the FICO® credit score that's used by many lenders to evaluate consumer credit risk. Scores calculated by credit reporting agencies from models developed by Fair Isaac Corporation are commonly called FICO® scores. These scores are derived solely from the information available on credit reporting agency reports. For a fee, you can obtain your FICO® score online at *www.myfico.com*.

Each of the credit reporting agencies (Experian, Equifax, and TransUnion) maintains a separate credit report on every consumer. In conjunction with this credit report, each has a corresponding credit score. The information on each credit report is often slightly different, because not all creditors and lenders report data to all three credit bureaus. Thus, when you review your three credit reports side by side, you'll often notice small discrepancies, which is totally normal. Because your credit score is calculated based upon the data on each credit report, each of your credits scores will also be slightly different.

When you apply for a major credit card or store credit card, that creditor will check your credit history by reviewing your credit report obtained from one of the credit reporting agencies. In many cases, when you're offered a credit decision in under five minutes, that decision was based exclusively on your credit score that went along with the credit report accessed. The quick approval or rejection was an automated decision.

When you apply for a more substantial loan, such as a car loan, the financing company will typically access all three of your credit reports, then use the middle credit score as a tool to help make an approval decision. If only two credit scores are available, which is not unusual, then the finance company will rely on the lower of the two.

Because the information on your credit report constantly changes, as creditors report new or updated data and old data (over seven years old) drops off your credit report, your credit score from each credit reporting agencies also changes. When your credit score is calculated, only data from your credit report is used. In other words, your credit score does *not* take the following data into account:

- Personal information, such as your sex, race, religion, nationality, or sexual orientation
- The value of your personal assets
- Your checking or savings account balances
- Your income

Because your credit score is considered an extremely reliable indication of your creditworthiness, it can be used to make auto loan decisions extremely fast. A creditor or lender can obtain your credit score in a matter of seconds and then often make an approval decision in just minutes, which is something that would have been impossible before, without the use of credit scores.

Driving Smart

Because credit scores are calculated by a computer using only information that appears in your credit report, there is little or no room for human biases in the decision-making process. Thus, it's much harder for a lender or creditor to discriminate against someone based on gender, race, religion, nationality, marital status, or sexual orientation.

Your credit score is an important number that you need to protect. Making irresponsible or bad financial decisions, paying late, applying for too much credit, and various other factors can all work against you and dramatically lower your credit score. Remember: not only will your credit score help to determine whether or not you're granted credit or a loan, it'll also directly help to determine what interest rate and fees you pay when using credit or taking out a loan. Having a credit score below average will cost you a lot of money now and in the future, because you will be paying much higher interest rates than someone with excellent credit.

Your credit score is *not* an arbitrary number. Each of the three credit reporting agencies (credit bureaus) uses its own formula to calculate credit scores, although the final scores you earn from each credit bureau will carry equal weight, no matter which agency calculates it.

Using a proprietary mathematical formula that is modified as consumer trends change, your credit score is calculated based on the following criteria:

Your payment history—This takes into account your payment information on specific types of loans, including your mortgage, current and past auto loans, credit cards, retail accounts, etc. It also takes into account any negative information listed in the public records section of your credit report, such as a bankruptcy, judgments, lawsuits, liens, wage attachments, collection items, etc. Within the calculation, your score is impacted not only by the number of late payments listed on your credit report, but also by the amount past due and how late you paid. On the positive side, your credit score will get a boost for each current account that's listed as "paid as agreed."

The amounts you owe—This takes into account the amount of money you owe on accounts, the types of accounts, the number of accounts you have with balances, the portion of each credit line used, and the portion of installment loan amounts still owing.

The length of your credit history—This is the time since each account was opened and the length of time since the last activity on the account.

New credit—The number of newly opened accounts, the number of recent credit inquiries, the time since your last new accounts were opened, and the time since the most recent inquiries were made are all taken into account.

Types of credit used—Also calculated into your credit score are the number of accounts and the type of accounts listed on your credit report: car loans, mortgages, credit cards, etc.

All of this information is taken into account in calculating your credit score or FICO® score. Depending on your overall credit profile, the amount of weight each piece of information or data is given will vary dramatically from person to person; however, your positive or negative payment history is typically weighted the heaviest when your credit score is calculated. Thus, late payments and other negative information will lower your score and maintaining or re-establishing a positive history (in terms of timely payments) will boost your score.

Driving Smart

Your payment history and amounts owned represent about 65 percent of your FICO® Score.

Obtaining Your Credit Report and Credit Score

Using the Internet, you can request and obtain a copy of your credit report from each of the three credit reporting agencies in under five minutes. Visit the official Annual Credit Report Request Service's Web site (*www.annualcreditreport.com*), select your home state, and complete the brief online form.

You'll be asked to provide your full name, date of birth, Social Security number, and current address. If you've lived at your current address for less than two years, you'll also be asked for your previous address. At the bottom of the on-screen questionnaire, you'll see a security code in a multicolored box. At the appropriate prompt, enter this security code and click the "Next" icon to continue.

You will now be prompted to select one or more of the three credit reporting companies from which to request your free credit report. Using your mouse, place an on-screen check mark next to one, two, or all three—Experian, Equifax, and TransUnion. Then, click on the "Next" icon located in the lower-right corner of the screen.

At this point, you will be transferred to the Web site of each credit reporting agency, one at a time, to obtain your free credit report. Once you've obtained each report and printed it out, click on the "Return to AnnualCreditReport.com" icon at the top of the screen. Then, from the *AnnualCreditReport.com* Web site you'll be redirected to the Web site of another credit reporting agency, if you've requested a report from that agency.

On each credit reporting agency's Web site, you'll be asked a few additional security questions to verify your identity. For example, you may be asked a question like "According to your credit profile, you may have opened a mortgage loan in or around [insert month and year]. Please select the lender to whom you currently make your mortgage payments. If you do not have a mortgage, select 'NONE OF THE ABOVE/DOES NOT APPLY.'" You'll then be provided with four or five options. Be prepared to answer three to five security questions when visiting each of the credit reporting agencies' Web sites.

After you answer the security questions correctly, your credit report will promptly be displayed on the computer screen. Choose the "Print Your Report" option to view a printer-friendly version of your credit report.

TIP: You can also request your credit reports by telephone by calling (877) 322-8228 or by mail (Annual Credit Report Request Service, P.O. Box 105281, Atlanta, GA 30348-5281), but it takes much longer.

WARNING: There are many companies that will advertise free credit reports, but you'll wind up having to join a credit monitoring service (for a fee) in order to access your reports. Only the Annual Credit Report Request Service is the official service for obtaining free copies of your credit report from Experian, TransUnion, and Equifax. Avoid contacting companies with similar and misleading names and Web site URLs.

The Cost of Obtaining Additional or More Frequent Credit Reports

If you want to obtain copies of your credit report more frequently than once every 12 months, there are several ways to do this. You can purchase single copies of your report from each of the credit reporting agencies or you can subscribe to a credit monitoring service, which includes unlimited access to your credit report (and potentially your credit score) for a monthly fee.

For a fee of up to $9.50 each, to purchase single copies of your credit report from each of the three credit reporting agencies, contact them directly:

Equifax: (800) 685-1111, www.equifax.com
Experian: (888) 397-3742, www.experian.com
TransUnion: (800) 916-8800, www.transunion.com

The consumer division of each of these credit reporting agencies also offers online credit monitoring services and the ability to purchase copies of your credit report with a corresponding credit score. For an additional fee, you can also obtain a three-in-one credit report—information from all three credit reporting agencies on one report. Some of these three-in-one reports also include your credit scores.

What About Your Credit Score?

In addition to the credit report that's compiled by each of the three credit reporting agencies, each also calculates your credit score. While you're entitled to a free copy of your credit report every 12 months, the credit reporting agencies are not obligated to provide you with your credit score for free. Instead, they charge you to obtain it. At the time you request a free copy of your credit report, you may receive an offer to purchase your corresponding credit score and receive the report and score at the same time. For this, you'll be charged approximately $6.00 per score.

You can also contact each of the three credit reporting agencies separately (using the contact information in the previous section) to purchase your credit score in conjunction with a credit report or separately. For example, from Experian, you can purchase a single credit report with the credit score for $15.00 or just the credit score for $5.95.

Driving Smart

It's definitely a good idea to purchase your credit score when you obtain a copy of your credit report. Simply by reviewing your credit report, it's virtually impossible for you to calculate or even estimate your corresponding credit score, yet this is a vital piece of information that will ultimately determine whether or not you're creditworthy. When obtaining your credit score, make sure what you're getting is a genuine *FICO® score*, since this is the number that at least 70 percent of all creditors and lenders use to make their approval decisions.

The Benefits of a Three-in-One Credit Report and How to Obtain One

Many companies, including the three major credit reporting agencies, offer comprehensive, three-in-one credit reports. On one report, you receive detailed information from all three credit agencies. This enables you to review and compare content from all three reports at once quickly and without having to flip among the three reports as you analyze your current situation. The price you pay for a three-in-one report will vary, based on the company you use to retrieve it and whether or not the corresponding credit scores are included. Expect to pay between $30.00 and $40.00 for a single three-in-one credit report, plus a little extra if you want your credit scores.

If you are extremely interested in tracking your credit report and credit score on an ongoing basis, subscribing to a credit monitoring service is a worthwhile investment. For example, TransUnion offers unlimited access to your constantly updated three-in-one credit report (with corresponding credit scores) and notifies you anytime a change is made to your credit report. This optional credit monitoring service costs $24.95 for the first month and then $14.95 per month thereafter.

The data provided on a three-in-one credit report will be identical to the data you'd receive by requesting separate credit reports from all three credit reporting agencies. The difference is in how the data is formatted.

Driving Smart

GET YOUR CREDIT REPORT FREE When you apply for an auto loan at a dealership, ask for a copy of your three-in-one credit report that they acquire. This is a way for you to obtain a copy of this report at no cost, because it's paid for by the dealership or auto finance company.

MAKE SURE IT'S LEGIT Before ordering a credit report, a three-in-one credit report, or credit monitoring service from a company other than the three major credit reporting agencies (credit bureaus), make sure the company is legitimate. You will need to provide personal information, including your name, date of birth, address, and Social Security number, which is data that could easily be used for identity theft or other fraudulent purposes.

UNLIMITED ACCESS When shopping for a credit monitoring service, ideally you want to receive unlimited access to your three-in-one credit report, with accompanying credit scores, for the lowest monthly fee possible. Some service offer one month free and then begin charging. Others charge extra for your credit scores. Before signing up for a service, make sure you understand what's included and what it costs. Also, determine if there's a start-up fee or a cancellation fee. For a monthly fee of $24.95 for the first month and $14.95 thereafter, TrueCredit (*www.truecredit.com*) offers unlimited access to all three of your credit reports and credit scores and allows you to automatically receive notifications any time changes are made to your credit report that impact your credit score.

Improve Your Credit Score Before Applying for Financing

Because your credit report and your credit score directly impact your ability to obtain financing and get competitive financing deals from car dealerships, your bank or credit union, or another lender, it's important that you make every effort to raise your credit score as high as possible before applying for an auto loan.

If you discover you need to improve your credit score before applying for an auto loan or if you apply for a loan and don't get approved, the following are five strategies that will help you boost your credit score within three to 12 months, depending on how badly damaged your credit score is and what caused that damage. Changes to your credit report can take up to 30 to 45 days, so plan accordingly.

Strategy #1: Pay Your Bills on Time

This strategy may seem extremely obvious, yet late payments are the most common piece of negative information that appears on credit reports and that can cause significant drops in credit scores. With loans and credit cards, it's vital that you always make at least the minimum monthly payments in a timely manner, each and every month, with no exceptions.

Your credit score is calculated based on a complex formula using your payment history, the amounts owed, the length of your credit history, any new credit, the types of credit you've used, and the number of credit inquiries made about your history. As mentioned earlier, your payment history is weighted the heaviest in this calculation, with late payments, collection accounts, defaulted loans, repossessions, and other negative payment history information all working against you and causing your credit score to drop.

Driving Smart

Paying all of your bills on time for at least six months in a row will raise your credit score. This applies to bills for which the creditor or lender reports payment information to the credit bureaus.

Strategy #2: Keep Your Credit Card Balances Low

The fact that you have credit cards impacts your credit score. Likewise, your payment history on those credit card accounts also impacts your score. Another factor in the calculation of your credit score is your credit card balances. Having a balance that represents 35 percent or more of your overall available credit limit on each card will actually hurt you, even if you make all of your payments on time and consistently pay more than the minimums due. If you have a $1,000 credit limit on a credit card, ideally you want to maintain a balance of less than $350 and also make timely monthly payments above the required minimums.

Strategy #3: Don't Close Accounts You're No Longer Using

One of the factors considered when calculating your credit score is the length of time you've had each credit account. You benefit from having a positive, long history with each creditor, even if the account is inactive or not used. The longer your positive credit history with each creditor, the better.

Avoid closing older and unused accounts. If you have credit cards you never use, simply put them in a safe place and forget about them. You don't want to have too many accounts open, but having five or six accounts open can be beneficial, even though you use only two or three cards.

Strategy #4: Apply for Credit Only When You Need It, Then Get the Best Rates

Retailers of appliances or other big-ticket items will often offer shoppers a discount and a good financing deal if they open a charge or credit card account with that retailer. Before applying for a store credit card, read the fine print. What's the interest rate? What fees are charged?

Apply for new credit only if you absolutely need it. If you have a credit card that you could use, applying for a retail store card you're going to use once or twice might not be a good idea. Applying for and obtaining multiple credit cards (including store credit cards) within a period of several months will be detrimental to your credit score. Unless you can save significantly on your purchase over time and can justify accepting a reduction in your credit score, don't apply for credit you don't actually need.

Strategy #5: Correct Inaccuracies in Your Credit Reports and Remove Old Information

One of the fastest and easiest ways to boost your credit score is to review all three of your credit reports carefully and correct any erroneous or outdated information. If you spot incorrect information, you can initiate a dispute and potentially have it corrected or removed within ten to 30 days.

You must be able to show that the information is inaccurate. Otherwise, negative information will remain on your credit report for seven years unless you negotiate with your individual creditors or lenders to remove that information.

Driving Smart

For more information about credit reports, including dozens of tips and strategies for improving your credit score, pick up a copy of *Dirty Little Secrets: What the Credit Bureaus Won't Tell You* (Entrepreneur Press).

Determine the Interest Rate and Financing Terms for Which You Qualify

Once you know your credit score, you can do some research online to figure out the best loan rates for which that score qualifies you. You'll find that interest rates and loan fees will vary dramatically, so if you know your score and then shop around for the best deals, you can save money.

The BankRate.com (*www.bankrate.com*) Web site is an online service that takes a national survey of auto loan lenders each week and reports the best new and used car financing

Driving Smart

NEGOTIATE! Don't just accept whatever loan rate and terms a dealership offers. Try negotiating. You might be able to get a more competitive rate or better terms working with a bank, a credit union, or another lender.

deals found. On this site, you can select your state, city, and loan term (36, 48, 60, or 72 months) and then choose new or used car financing to find current rates for someone with an average or better credit score. You'll probably discover that if there are five to ten banks or finance companies listed, there will be a discrepancy of as much as two full percentage points in the interest rates being offered. This is why it pays to shop around for the best rates.

Driving Smart

CALCULATORS YOU CAN USE The Bankrate.com Web site has an auto loan calculator that you can use to calculate the monthly payment on a loan if you provide the loan amount, term (number of months), and interest rate. The Yahoo! Auto site (*autos.yahoo.com/finance/loan-calc/*) and many other car-related Web sites have similar calculators.

RAISE THAT SCORE To ensure that you'll qualify for the best rates and experience the least trouble getting approval for an auto loan without a co-signer, work on raising your credit score above 650. Your chances of obtaining approval will improve if you can make a down payment of at least 20 percent on the vehicle and then finance no more than 80 percent of the purchase price.

Shop Around for the Best Financing Options

After you've selected the vehicle you want to purchase and have selected a dealership, you can shop around for the best rates by completing a loan application with the dealership. Most dealers have relationships with many lenders and can quickly shop around to get your loan approved. However, a dealership will *not* necessarily offer you the lowest interest rate and loan fees for which you'd qualify. You'll probably want to negotiate a little with the dealership and then contact one or more banks, credit unions, or other lenders for better rates and terms.

If you already know your credit score, most lenders will be able to give you over the telephone an idea of the loan interest rates they could offer, without asking you to complete a full application. However, no financing company will guarantee a rate until it actually processes your application and can approve it.

You can also shop for auto financing via the Internet. There are many services, including Bankrate.com, that enable you to find the best rates from local banks and lenders and then complete an application online. To begin shopping for competitive auto financing on the Internet, use any search engine (e.g., Google or Yahoo!) and enter the search phrase "auto loan." If you have a low credit score, you can use the search phrase "bad credit auto financing." Information about a handful of car-related Web sites, including several that can help you shop for a competitive loan, can be found in Chapters 5 and 8.

Vehicle Financing Options for People with Bad Credit

If you have poor credit, you have four main options for obtaining auto financing:

1. Try to improve your credit score *before* applying for a loan. How long it'll take to achieve a significant improvement will depend on the negative information currently on your credit report and the steps you take to change it. You may have to wait for six months or more to purchase or lease a vehicle.

2. Accept the fact that you'll be paying a significantly higher interest rate and higher fees if you can find a lender that will approve your loan immediately. You'll also most likely need to pay at least 20 percent down. The bigger the down payment you're willing and able to make, especially if your credit is below average, the better your chances of getting approval.

3. Find someone with good credit to co-sign your loan. This means that he or she will take responsibility for the loan if you default on the payments. If you make payments late or default on the loan, it will damage your co-signer's credit score as well as your own.

4. Save up and buy a car with cash, so you don't need any financing. You may find that in your current financial sit-

uation it makes more sense to purchase an inexpensive used car right now. You can then work toward improving your credit score and then, in a few months, obtain financing to purchase a new vehicle.

Now that you're aware of your current credit situation and can determine whether or not you'll qualify for a loan, you can focus on deciding if purchasing a car is in your future or rather if it makes more sense to lease. The next chapter focuses on the pros and cons of buying new and buying used. If you think leasing might be a viable option for you, be sure to check out Chapter 6.

CHAPTER 3

New vs. Used: Finding the Best Vehicle for You

WHAT'S IN THIS CHAPTER

- Should you buy new or used?
- How your budget will impact the decision between new and used
- The scoop on certified pre-owned vehicles
- How and where to shop for the best price

Buy or Lease a Car Without Getting Taken for a Ride

As you already know, buying or leasing a car means making a lot of important decisions, based on your wants, needs, and budget. You'll need to make decisions relating to the following:

1. The make, model, and year of the vehicle you wish to purchase or lease
2. Whether to trade in or sell your current vehicle
3. Financing
4. Insurance

Many dealerships will try to get you to consider some or all of these decisions at the same time, in order to confuse you and so they can make the most money. However, it's in your best interest financially to handle each of these steps separately. First, shop around and negotiate the best price for the vehicle you want. Next, negotiate the value of your trade-in separately or consider selling it privately. Third, shop around and negotiate the best financing rates. Finally, shop around for the best insurance rates and coverage.

One of the most important decisions you'll have to make when deciding on the vehicle to buy is whether to buy new or used. Typically, this is a decision based mainly on your finances. It also has to do with the amount of peace of mind you want. This concept of "peace of mind" will be explored later, because it's like insurance coverage in terms of protecting yourself against things going wrong with the vehicle. The better the warranty and the newer the vehicle, the more peace of mind, because the less chance you'll have to pay for costly repairs.

Driving Smart

RISK AND REWARD Buying a used vehicle always involves some level of risk, because you don't know how it was driven or maintained by the pervious owner(s). Some used vehicles come with a warranty, although it may be honored only by the dealership that sells you the vehicle, not the manufacturer or other dealerships.

What you'll discover from this chapter is that even if you can afford a new vehicle, you'll probably be able to get much more vehicle for your money if you buy a used or *certified pre-owned (CPO) vehicle* from a reputable dealership. In fact, for less than half the price of an average, low or mid-priced, bare-bones new car (one with few options), you can usually purchase a larger, more luxurious, and well-loaded used vehicle.

CAR SPEAK **CERTIFIED PRE-OWNED (CPO)**—This is the current term for "reconditioned and used." Authorized dealerships take their off-lease vehicles—vehicles that have been leased and are usually less than five years old—and put them through an inspection process, attach an extended warranty and other perks, and sell them. Many luxury car manufacturers have established CPO sales departments at their dealerships. A recent study conducted by J.D. Powers and Associates determined that CPO vehicles accounted for 41 percent of all used-car dealership sales in 2005.

This chapter explores the pros and cons of buying new, used, or CPO. If you decide to purchase a new vehicle, the information offered in Chapter 4 will be extremely helpful. If

Driving Smart

USED = SAVINGS According to research conducted by CNW Marketing Research, the average sale price of a new car in 2005 was $26,741 and the average price of a used vehicle was only $9,832. If you're shopping for a used vehicle, you must do additional research and take extra precautions (as you'll learn in Chapter 5), but the savings can be well worth the extra effort.

you opt to acquire a used or CPO vehicle, Chapter 5 contains information to help you get the best deal possible and avoid the many problems associated with acquiring a used vehicle. In Chapter 6, you'll learn all about your other option, leasing.

Your goal should be to acquire a vehicle that will satisfy all of your needs and desires, provide the maximum amount of comfort and safety, be reliable, and fit your finances at the start and as you make the monthly payments and cover all of the other costs associated with driving a vehicle.

Should You Buy New or Used?

The decision between new and used is definitely personal.

Buying a *new* vehicle will almost always cost you more money, but there are some concrete benefits. For example, a new car will cost less for maintenance and repairs, at least for the first several years of ownership, while the manufacturer's warranty is in effect. For the first several years, you'll typically need to pay only for oil changes and other low-cost routine maintenance.

Other benefits of buying a new vehicle are that you can easily select your color, pick your configuration and options, and know that the car is equipped with the latest safely features and most technologically advanced gadgets available. You can also take advantage of rebates and incentives offered by the manufacturer or dealership to save money. The interest rate you'll pay to finance a new vehicle will also typically be lower than to finance a used vehicle.

Thanks to the continued popularity of certified pre-owned vehicle programs offered by almost all vehicle manufacturers, it's now possible to buy a *used vehicle* that's "like new" and save significant money. As you'd expect, however, there are pros and cons associated with buying a used vehicle.

TIP: If you're shopping for a used vehicle, you'll have an abundance of choices. The selection of used cars on the market is far greater than the selection of new vehicles. This gives you more choices and negotiating power. According to CNW Marketing Research, in 2005, more than 44.1 million used cars were sold, while only 17 million new vehicles were sold. Approximately 1.4 million of the used vehicles sold were classified as *certified pre-owned*.

Focus on Your Budget and Your Needs

Some people simply don't want to buy a used vehicle, no matter what. They'll only consider buying new. They're willing to spend the extra money because they don't want to "inherit someone else's problems" and they want total control over how the vehicle is configured. Perhaps they also like that "new car smell" and the feeling of being the first to sit in the driver's seat of a vehicle. Buying a new vehicle also offers the ultimate peace of mind, because for the life of the manufacturer's warranty (and any extended warranty), most if not all major repairs will be covered. In some cases, the decision to purchase a new vehicle is purely emotional: you fall in love with a specific car make and model and immediately decide it's the vehicle you'd like to own.

If you can afford to have this mindset, that's great: there are certainly plenty of options available when shopping for a new vehicle. However, if money is tight, you can potentially save a lot of money shopping for a used vehicle.

Driving Smart

TEMPER YOUR EMOTIONS It's extremely common for people to make their car-buying decisions based purely on emotions. They find a car they love and then that's the only car they'll consider. It's always smart to look at comparable vehicles from other manufacturers. But if you have your heart set on a specific make and model, at least invest the time to shop around for the best price and financing options. Don't just purchase the first vehicle you see from the first dealership you visit.

If you can afford $15,000 to $25,000 or more for a vehicle (with financing), you can buy either new or used. (It's decision time again!) It's important to understand that if you buy used, you can afford a vehicle with more of the features, options, and accessories you want, especially if you shop around for one in pristine, "like new" condition with a good warranty.

If, however, your budget for a vehicle (with financing) is small, say under $15,000, the decision between new and used is pretty much made for you. The less money you have to spend for a used vehicle, the more research you'll want to do in order to find a reputable dealership. You'll then need to do general research on the make and model of vehicle you decide to buy, plus more research about the specific vehicle you're interested in purchasing to make sure you'll be happy with your decision over the long term.

When buying an inexpensive used car or a car that's several years old with high mileage, it becomes very important to research that specific vehicle by obtaining its history report (from Carfax, for example). You want a car that's reliable and not already in need of major repairs, so you don't get stuck with significant repair bills shortly after you acquire it.

Through research, you want to find a used car that will offer you not only the features and functionality you want and need, but also as much peace of mind as possible. More than half of all people buying used vehicles focus on the warranty. Make sure the warranty you're receiving (if any) will be honored by the vehicle's manufacturer and not just by the dealership that sells you the vehicle.

You might also consider paying a bit extra for a *bumper-to-bumper* warranty, the most comprehensive, as opposed to just a *powertrain* warranty, which covers only the engine, transmission, and other parts of the drive train (the components that transmit power from the engine to the wheels, including clutch, transmission, drive shafts or axle shafts, and differential).

Whether you opt for new or used, focus on what's important to you in terms of vehicle functionality, space, safety features, and comfort. Then, figure out what you can afford and how you can get the best vehicle for your money.

If New, Pay Attention to Residual Values and Depreciation

For some new car buyers, residual or resale value is an extremely important factor in choosing a vehicle. Some vehicles will have significantly higher residual values than others. For example, you may be deciding between two comparably priced new vehicles (priced at $25,000). You also know you plan to sell the vehicle in three years. Based on your research, you determine that in three years, one of the vehicles will most likely be worth $15,000, while the other will only be worth $11,000. Thus, for that second vehicle, it'll cost you $4,000 more to own it, because you'll be able to sell or trade it in for less money in the future.

RESIDUAL VALUE—This is the worth of a vehicle at a given time, the difference between the purchase price and the amount of *depreciation*.   **CAR SPEAK**

DEPRECIATION—This is the loss of value of a vehicle over a given time. A vehicle begins depreciating as soon as it's purchased and driven off the lot. In the first two years, the value of a new vehicle will drop

---

at least 30 percent, sometimes significantly more, depending on the make, model, and year. What it is worth at any given time is the *residual value*. Through research, you can determine the expected residual value of a specific new vehicle after two, three, or five years. To research depreciation and residual values of new vehicles, you can visit many of the popular car-related Web sites, including Cars.com.

Driving Smart

USED PRICES If you purchase a used vehicle, you don't have to worry about depreciation or residual value, because the vehicle has already lost a significant amount of its value within its first year or two. The price you pay for a used vehicle will likely be based on its residual value or depreciation.

Disadvantages of a Used Vehicle

While there are definite potential advantages to buying a used vehicle, there are also potential disadvantages. You can easily avoid many of these potential problems, however, by doing research in advance and buying from a reputable dealership or owner.

As you'll learn in Chapter 5, when researching a used vehicle, you should learn as much as possible about the make, model, and year of the vehicle, including its resale value, reliability, safety record, and consumer satisfaction record. Then, once you find a specific used vehicle that interests you, you should research that vehicle by independently obtaining a vehicle history report. (Never rely on a report provided by the dealership or seller.) You want to know who has owned that vehicle, how it has been treated, what major repair work has been done, whether it's been in any accidents, and, if so, whether it's been classified as "totaled" or "salvaged" and then rebuilt. You'll also want to pay attention to any warranty being offered. Are you still eligible to be covered by the manufacturer's warranty or will you be relying on a warranty provided by a dealership? What's covered by the warranty and what major repair work will be required in the future?

For vehicles that are older or that have higher mileage, you'll need to check whether the timing belt has been replaced, the condition of the tires, whether the brakes and exhaust system will need to be repaired or replaced, the condition of the transmission, and the overall condition of the exterior (body) and interior. Replacing a timing belt, for example, can cost $300 to $600, while putting new tires on the car can cost $300 total to $200 or more per tire.

Driving Smart

WARRANTY NOT WORRY A warranty takes much of the worry out of buying a used vehicle. Typically, any remaining coverage from a new-car warranty usually transfers to the new owner. If you're buying from a dealership, an extended warranty will then typically take effect when the original warranty expires. (Make sure this is the case!) Much like the original warranty, extended coverage on a used car typically lasts a certain number of years or miles, whichever occurs first. Extended warranties will vary dramatically depending on the manufacturer and dealership. Luxury brands, such as Mercedes-Benz, Jaguar, BMW, or Volvo, for example, tend to offer more comprehensive extended warranties than other brands.

The honesty and reliability of the dealership is also an important consideration. Just about everyone knows about the negative stereotypes associated with used car salespeople and how they'll say or do almost anything to sell a vehicle. You definitely want to find a dealer that does *not* work based up on this negative stereotype.

Driving Smart

DON'T ASSUME Make sure you understand what's covered by an extended warranty. Don't assume it's a bumper-to-bumper warranty. Also, pay attention to when the warranty expires. Is it based on the time *you* own the vehicle and the mileage *you* put on it or is it based on the total age of the vehicle and the total mileage? For example, if the warranty is for four years or 50,000 miles, but the car is three years old and has 40,000 miles, that warranty will remain in effect for only one more year or 10,000 miles more, whichever comes first. After that, you're paying for any repairs.

GET IT INSPECTED Before purchasing any used vehicle, especially from the current owner, have the vehicle carefully inspected by an independent mechanic you trust. This might cost you $100 or more, but you could save thousands if the vehicle turns out to be in poor condition or a lemon. Again, don't rely on appearances, a drive around the block, or what the seller tells you about the vehicle. Get an expert's opinion.

Certified Pre-Owned Vehicles Are Very Good Options

A certified pre-owned vehicle (CPO) is a wonderful alternative to a new or used vehicle. It's an excellent way to save money and get more for your money.

As explained earlier, a CPO is a used vehicle that has been selected by an expert at an authorized dealership, put through rigorous testing and refurbishment, professionally detailed and cleaned, and than given a manufacturer's warranty. Thus, the vehicle is transformed into "like new" condition and receives the manufacturer's seal of approval.

Typically, a CPO is less than five years old and has fewer than 50,000 to 60,000 miles. In many cases, it was a leased vehicle. Because the manufacturer or its authorized dealership has inspected and fully refurbished the vehicle and offers a manufacturer's warranty, the price of a CPO vehicle is always higher than for a comparable uncertified vehicle. In fact, the price could be between $1,000 and $3,000 higher. For that extra money, you're paying for peace of mind, knowing that the CPO has passed inspection and comes with a warranty that will be honored by the manufacturer, not just an individual dealership.

While a CPO will cost more than an uncertified used vehicle, it will be significantly less expensive than buying a new vehicle, especially for a mid- to high-priced (luxury) vehicle.

Driving Smart

CPO CHECKLISTS Every manufacturer has its own comprehensive checklist for certifying a used vehicle. This checklist will contain between 100 and 300 specific items, depending on the manufacturer. Audi, for example, has a checklist of more than 300 points. If you ask, a CPO dealer will provide you with the manufacturer's checklist and warranty information.

So, if you're considering buying a used vehicle, by paying the premium for a CPO, you're basically buying insurance against the expense of many types of costly repairs in the future, plus you'll be receiving many of the perks and benefits associated with purchasing a new vehicle from the authorized dealership.

Almost every major vehicle manufacturer offers a certified pre-owned vehicle program through its authorized dealerships. Each manufacturer's program is slightly different and offers customers different perks and benefits.

For example, here's what Lexus offers, according to its Web site: "Each Lexus Certified Pre-Owned Vehicle is specifically chosen by a Lexus dealer and their team of experts. Next, Lexus-trained technicians perform a meticulous inspection. Only those models that meet the highest standards are then given a Lexus-backed, three-year/100,000-total-vehicle-mile warranty that begins on your date of purchase. As the new buyer of a CPO vehicle, you are entitled to the privileges of Lexus ownership such as Roadside Assistance, a complimentary loaner car and Trip Interruption services."

When visiting an authorized dealership, be sure to inquire about the availability of CPO vehicles and compare all of your

Driving Smart

LUXURY CPO To learn more about the care and effort put into refurbishing a luxury vehicle by the manufacturer and authorized dealer, the Lexus Web site offers an excellent tutorial about CPOs. Go to *www.lexus.com/cpodemystify* to learn more about the many benefits of buying a CPO.

options when considering purchasing a new vehicle. Financially, a CPO could make a lot of sense for most people, especially if you're hoping to purchase a fully loaded vehicle with many costly options and features.

Driving Smart

LOW PRICE LUXURY One of the biggest advantages of buying a CPO is that you can typically afford a higher class of vehicle or get a comparable late-model vehicle for less than the price of buying new. This often allows car shoppers to look at more upscale brands, like Lexus, Audi, Volvo, or Mercedes-Benz, which they could not have afforded otherwise.

By purchasing a CPO, you avoid the depreciation loss associated with buying a new vehicle, which drops in value the moment it's driven off the dealership's lot and continues to drop significantly during the first two or three years of ownership. Discounts on financing, other manufacturer or dealer incentives, and the manufacturer's extended warranty make CPO vehicles very attractive.

How and Where to Shop for the Best Price

In shopping for a car, whether new or used, you have many options. Ideally, you should start the process by completing the questionnaires and checklists in this book to determine your wants and needs and then use the Internet to help you identify a specific make, model, and year. (Chapter 7 describes some of the best sources on the Internet for research on cars and shopping for cars.) You'll then want to start looking at ads online and in newspapers and magazines, visiting dealerships, attending car shows, and finding other ways to inspect and test-drive vehicles.

If you want to get the best deal possible, nothing can replace research and the need to visit more than one dealership or negotiate with more than one owner. You probably won't get the best deal or save money if you purchase the very first vehicle you find that's suitable or with which you develop an emotional bond.

Driving Smart

GETTING QUOTES Once you know the make, model, and year you want and you've decided on options and features, you can obtain price quotes from dealers over the telephone or online—without having to visit them in person. The potential drawback to this is that you won't always get the lowest price right away. You'll still need to negotiate. Many dealerships are reluctant to negotiate their absolute best price over the phone or via e-mail. You can, however, compare asking prices for vehicles from multiple dealerships by requesting quotes online or over the phone. If the initial quote is competitive, you can always visit that dealership in person to negotiate further.

AUCTIONS Vehicle auctions are another option for acquiring a vehicle at a good price, but this is recommended only for someone extremely familiar with cars in general, since you can't always test-drive a vehicle being sold at auction.

Also, never allow yourself to be rushed or bullied by a salesperson or anyone at the dealership. You'll often be told that several other people are looking at the same vehicle as you, so you need to decide fast and put a deposit down immediately. Don't fall for this line! Never put a deposit on any vehicle until you're reasonably sure it's the one you want to buy. Chances are good that if someone else purchases the vehicle, the dealership will be able to get an identical vehicle quickly—if there's not another already in stock.

Take your time! Get answers to all of your questions. Be sure you're working within your time frame, not the dealership's timeframe. Do all of the necessary research. Negotiate your best price and then consult with two or three other dealers to see if you can get a better price. Remember: buying a car is a decision that should be based on finances, not only emotions. Also focus on practicality and necessity.

TIP: Chapter 8 features interviews with car experts, including a senior analyst with Kelley Blue Book and the senior editor of Autobytel.com, who share valuable advice and insight on buying a car and then negotiating the best price possible, whether you're working with a dealership or a private seller.

Is a New Vehicle in Your Future?

If you determine you're interested in acquiring a new car and you can afford it, you'll benefit from the next chapter, which offers valuable information on shopping for a new car. As you're about to discover, the process of buying new differs slightly from the process of buying used. Leasing is a totally different process altogether, which you'll learn more about in Chapter 6.

CHAPTER 4

Buying a New Car

WHAT'S IN THIS CHAPTER

- The steps involved in buying a new car
- Finding the new car you want
- Understanding how new cars are priced
- Negotiating your best price
- The hidden costs to consider

Buy or Lease a Car Without Getting Taken for a Ride

Buying a new car can be fun and exciting, but it can also be confusing and frustrating. After all, you have to make a handful of important decisions before selecting the vehicle you purchase and then you probably want to get the best deal possible. Yet, no matter how hard they negotiate, most people wind up feeling like they could have done better. They may be happy with their purchase decision, but still feel that perhaps they paid too much or got talked into buying options or an extended warrantee, for example, that they simply didn't need or want.

Part of this feeling comes from the reputation that car salespeople have for being fast talkers, tough negotiators, and at times outright dishonest. Of course, not all car salespeople fit this image. However, finding someone who doesn't and who also works for a reputable dealership can be a challenge. Add to this the fact that most people shopping for a new vehicle know little or nothing about cars, so they may get bogged down by all of the fancy buzzwords for vehicles and features. After they've decided on a vehicle make and model, they still need to get financing.

As you already know, the very best way to begin the process of buying a new car is with research. Define your needs and wants. Next, learn about vehicles that fit your needs. After that, figure out what you can afford. Once you narrow down your choices to just a handful of makes and models, you can do additional research by visiting car-related Web sites, reading car magazines, attending car shows, and

Driving Smart

READ THE FINE PRINT Until you've selected the vehicle and the dealership, refrain from offering any dealer a deposit on any vehicle, filling out a loan application, or signing any paperwork you don't understand. (Always read everything carefully and ask questions.) As soon as you walk through the door of a dealership, a salesperson will attempt to sell you a vehicle as soon as possible. Never allow yourself to be rushed, bullied, or misled into making a decision you're not ready to make, no matter what the salesperson does or says. Take your time. If at any point you become uncomfortable in a dealership or with a salesperson, simply walk out. Almost always, you'll be able to find a comparable vehicle at a dealer for the same price or even lower.

visiting dealerships to take test-drives to further narrow down your options.

Car salespeople know all about how to deal with consumers who aren't too knowledgeable about cars, who appear to be uncomfortable negotiating, who haven't done their research, or who don't truly know what they can afford. These are the consumers salespeople can take advantage of most easily. Thus, it's important to be fully prepared before you begin working with any salesperson. If you haven't reviewed your budget and don't know what you can afford, a salesperson can tinker with the numbers and make an awful deal sound amazing. Remember: car salespeople have much more experience and training in this process than you.

A salesperson might offer you a vehicle for a very attractive monthly payment, but not focus on the fact that you'd be making that payment for five years and ultimately paying thousands of dollars in interest charges. That same salesperson might also attempt to sell you options and accessories you simply don't need or want by getting you caught up in the emotions and excitement involved in buying a new car.

Right from the start, a savvy salesperson will always try to get you to commit to something (even to buying a vehicle) and create a false sense of urgency. You'll hear lines like these: "If we can agree on a price right now, are you ready to purchase this vehicle and drive it away today?" and "I can check if we have the car in blue; if so, are you ready to buy it now?" and "If I can get your monthly payment down to $300, are you ready to make a deal?"

In terms of creating urgency, you might hear a salesperson say, "We only have one car like the one you want in stock and I have three other people currently looking at it. In fact, one person is coming in later today to buy it. I can give it to you, however, if you make a decision right now." You might also hear something like "I can offer you this special deal today only. If you come back tomorrow, the price or the financing I'm offering you won't be available." About 90 percent of the time (or more) these statements are false or greatly overstated.

Driving Smart

DON'T TELL THEM WHAT YOU CAN AFFORD Offering a salesperson too much information about your personal financial situation and credit history too soon in the buying process can be detrimental. Once you fill out a loan application and the dealership pulls your credit reports, for example, the salesperson can calculate what you can afford—at least on paper. Those calculations do not take into account your other monthly expenses, such as mortgage and groceries, or that you need to pay for your child's college education. In fact, most salespeople don't care about these matters. If a salesperson perceives you have money and can afford a more expensive car than what you're interested in, he or she may try to sell you the most expensive vehicle you can afford or for which your credit score qualifies you. Only you know what down payment and monthly payment you can afford and are willing to make.

A good salesperson will look at how you're dressed (clothes and any jewelry), study your body language, and ask lots of questions in order to gauge your level of knowledge and your level of interest in buying a vehicle and to help determine what you can afford. A good salesperson will also notice the car you're driving currently and estimate its value, plus ask questions about your occupation, trips you've taken recently, any children, and your hobbies in order to help gauge your income level long before looking at your loan application or credit reports.

A salesperson will often gather as much information about you as possible, often subtly, in order to sell you the most expensive and profitable vehicle possible. Pay attention to the information you disclose through "casual conversation" and nonverbal communication. Questions that seem to be nothing more than friendly chatter could have another purpose altogether.

Driving Smart

DON'T DRESS UPSCALE When visiting a dealership to shop for a new car, don't dress up for the occasion. Leave your designer clothing and expensive jewelry at home. A savvy salesperson will know if you're wearing a $500 pair of shoes, a $1,500 outfit, or a $2,000 wristwatch, for example, and take advantage of this information. No matter how friendly a salesperson seems, remember that his or her job is to sell—as much as possible, as quickly as possible. The goal is often to unload vehicles that are currently on the lot and to make those vehicles most appealing to you, whether or not they meet your needs or fit your budget.

Once you start visiting dealerships, you'll notice that even after you've communicated what you intend to spend, the salesperson may try to sell you on a slightly more expensive vehicle or add costly options. If, for example, you mention early on that you can afford a $350 monthly payment or you want a vehicle priced under $23,000, the salesperson will typically start off by showing you a nicely equipped vehicle priced at $25,000 or that would have a monthly payment of

Driving Smart

GET IT IN WRITING Whenever a salesperson quotes a price or describes a vehicle feature, make sure these statements are backed up in writing. The vehicle's sales brochures (created by the manufacturer) will summarize important features and technical specifications. The research you do and the vehicle-specific reviews you read will help you verify facts and figures. Unless what's being offered is in writing, don't rely on it as fact. This strategy will help keep you from being misled or misinformed.

Driving Smart

DON'T PAY IN CASH Never pay a deposit in cash for a vehicle. If you opt to make a deposit once you decide to purchase a vehicle, pay the least possible and use a major credit card. Make sure the deposit is fully refundable if you change your mind.

$400. Thus, it's important to stay focused on what you need and on your budget, regardless of the sales pitch.

The Steps Involved with Buying a New Car

It's important to understand that buying a new vehicle is a process. If you're willing to be patient and follow all of the steps (without taking shortcuts or making hasty decisions driven by your emotions instead of common sense and hard facts), you're more apt to wind up getting the best deal possible on a vehicle that's most suited to your needs and wants.

While many of the steps involved in buying a new vehicle have already been discussed, they're listed here once again to show the big picture.

1. **Do research.** Use the Internet, read car magazines for reviews, and attend car shows, for example, to know what's available, learn about pricing, obtain information about safety and consumer satisfaction, and more accurately define your needs.

2. **Determine what you can afford.** Evaluate your overall budget—income, current living expenses, and debts—to

figure how much you can actually afford, not what your credit reports and credit score could qualify you to finance.

3. **Select a make and model.** Narrow down your choices—based on your wants and needs—to a handful of comparable vehicles. Start by choosing a vehicle category, such as an SUV or four-door sedan. Then, reduce your options to a few choices that fit your budget. You can do this online or by visiting dealerships and taking test-drives. As you're narrowing down your choices, research those specific makes and models; you can do this primarily online and with printed reviews.

4. **Customize the vehicle.** Select the manufacturer- and dealer-installed options, and accessories you want and need.

5. **Shop around for the best price.** After you've narrowed down your ideal vehicle to a specific make and model and decided on the exact configuration, it's time to prepare to negotiate the price. You can easily solicit quotes from dealerships in person, by phone, or online.

6. **Start negotiating.** Preparation is vital. Through online research, you can determine what others in your area have paid for the same vehicle and you can learn about current incentives and rebates.

7. **Negotiate your trade-in, if any.** Often, you'll get a higher price if you sell your existing vehicle privately, but this takes more time. Many people find it easier to trade in their vehicle. However, you should negotiate the value of your trade-in only after you've agreed on the price of the vehicle you're

purchasing. The value of your trade-in will then be deducted from that price.

CAR SPEAK   **TRADE-IN VALUE**—This is the amount a dealership credits a buyer for his or her current vehicle as partial payment for another vehicle. This amount is typically about five percent less than the wholesale market value of the trade-in vehicle. You can research the trade-in value and resale value of your current vehicle by using independent sources, such as *Kelley Blue Book* (*www.kbb.com*). This price is based on the make, model, year, mileage, resale value, and overall condition.

---

8. **Apply for financing.** Whether you apply through your dealership or with a bank or credit union or another lender, find the best rates you qualify for and the financing option with the lowest fees. Pay attention to the fees and charges, as well as the interest rate. Also, be prepared to make a down payment on the vehicle. This is an out-of-pocket expense. Most dealerships will accept cash, a certified check, a money order, a wire transfer, or a credit card.

Driving Smart

HIDDEN COSTS In addition to the length of the loan, fees, down payment, monthly payment, and interest rate (annual percentage rate, APR), pay careful attention to the terms of the loan. For example, consider things like grace periods for payments, fees for paying late, and pre-payment penalties. All of the financing terms should be clearly spelled out in writing. If you don't understand completely, don't sign the paperwork or even the loan application until you do.

---

9. **Complete the paperwork.** There's a lot of paperwork involved with purchasing a new car. Make sure that you have plenty of time, so you can read everything and get answers to all of your questions. Whatever you sign will become legally binding. All oral agreements—whether about the vehicle, the terms of the sale, or the financing—should be put in writing. Most dealers offer to acquire the title, license, registration, and inspection sticker on your behalf (for a fee). This will save you a lot of time and trouble.

10. **Obtain insurance.** Shop around for appropriate coverage and the best price. (Chapter 10 covers automotive insurance.)

Driving Smart

BUYER'S REMORSE Once all of the papers are signed, the new vehicle becomes yours legally. There's rarely an opportunity to return the vehicle if you experience buyer's remorse or change your mind, for whatever reason.

CHECK IT CAREFULLY Before taking possession of the new vehicle, inspect its exterior and interior thoroughly. Check for all the accessories and options you've paid for. Then take a test-drive. If there's a problem, bring it to the attention of the salesperson immediately. Do not take possession of the vehicle until the problem is resolved to your satisfaction.

Points to Consider When Choosing Your Vehicle

Narrowing down the choices to a specific make and model will require considering many factors, depending on what's important to you. The following is a list of things to consider once you've reduced the possibilities to a handful of comparable vehicles in a specific category.

- **Comfort.** How comfortable is the vehicle? Does it have the space, feel, and features to make your driving experience a pleasure?

- **Cost of Ownership.** Consider the ongoing costs, including gas, routine maintenance, repairs, insurance, parking, and taxes.

- **Consumer Satisfaction Ratings.** This is a rating for each make and model based on the overall experience of current owners of that make and model. It takes into account price, quality, safety, and overall happiness of current owners. J.D. Power and Associates (*www.jdpower.com*) is an independent company that produces these ratings for virtually all vehicle makes and models.

- **Current Vehicle Trade-in Value.** Dealers will offer more or less for your current vehicle, according to their need and desire to sell you that new vehicle. Your current vehicle's mileage, condition, and Blue Book value will all be taken into consideration as well.

- **Driving Experience.** This is a highly subjective consideration. Do you feel comfortable driving the vehicle? Do you feel safe? Do you believe the vehicle is a perfect match for you and your driving habits, needs, budget, and lifestyle?

- **Features and Functionality.** Whether it's an automatic transmission, anti-lock brakes, a GPS navigation system, leather seats, or a state-of-the-art audio system, you should consider the importance of standard features and options. Remember: what comes standard in one vehicle may be optional in an otherwise comparable vehicle.

- **Fuel Economy.** The estimates for miles per gallon for city and highway driving are an important consideration among consumers who drive a lot and who are concerned about the cost of gasoline.

Driving Smart

FUEL ECONOMY INFORMATION To learn which new vehicles get the best mileage, consult the free *Fuel Economy Guide* available from the U.S. Environmental Protection Agency (EPA) and the U.S. Department of Energy at *www.fueleconomy.gov/feg/feg2000.htm*.

- **Highway Crash Test and Rollover Ratings.** These are a measure of vehicle safety based on crash testing. These tests are regulated by the National Highway Traffic Safety Administration (NHTSA), which has created federal safety standards and regulations for automakers and their suppliers. To check the ratings for specific vehicles online, visit *www.safercar.gov*. This Web site offers information on all vehicle makes and models, starting with the 1990 model year.
- **LUXURY.** Many new vehicles are equipped with features for greater comfort, such as heated and/or multi-contour

Driving Smart

SAFETY CONCERNS If vehicle safety is a concern, download two free brochures published by the NHTSA, *Buying a Safer Car* and *Buying a Safer Car for Child Passengers*, from this Web page: *www.safercar.gov/pages/ ResourcesLinksBSC.htm*. These brochures will help you understand the published ratings for frontal crash tests and side-impact crash tests for any new vehicle. You'll also learn about seatbelts, anti-lock brake systems, electronic stability control, daytime running lights, tire pressure monitoring systems, front and side airbags, and other safety equipment in most new vehicles.

STAR RATINGS To help promote vehicle safety, starting September 1, 2007 (for all 2008 model year vehicles and beyond), all manufacturers are required to display the NHTSA's star rating test results for front and side crashes and non-destructive rollovers. These results will be displayed on the window price tags of all new vehicles. All three tests use a five-star rating system, with five stars being the safest. This new policy is called "Stars on Cars" and is being initiated by the NHTSA and the U.S. Department of Transportation.

seats, high-end audio or video systems, or dual climate control.

- **Price and Financing Options.** Comparable vehicles from different manufacturers are often priced differently, sometimes a difference of several thousand dollars in the base price. It's important to look at the total price of each vehicle and what it includes and what it does not include that would cost extra. When a manufacturer or a dealership offers special financing options, rebates, incentives, and special offers, these too can impact the price.

Buy or Lease a Car Without Getting Taken for a Ride

- **Published Reviews.** When a professional automotive journalist reviews a vehicle for a Web site, a newspaper, or a magazine, for example, that knowledge and insight can help you choose a vehicle. It's important to trust only reviews that are unbiased, thorough, timely, and from a reputable media outlet.

- **Rebates, Incentives, and Dealer Holdback.** In addition to finding out what the dealership paid for a vehicle and what other people in your area have recently paid for that vehicle or comparable vehicles, find out what *rebates*, *incentives*, and *dealer holdbacks* are currently being offered for the vehicle make and model. With this information, you could negotiate a price that's lower than the *invoice price*.

- **Resale/Residual Value.** If you plan to sell your vehicle in three or more years, it's important to know what it's expected to be worth at that time. Some vehicle makes and models retain their value much better than others. Some vehicles will have a residual value as much as 70 percent of the purchase price after three years (if in good condition), while other vehicles will have a residual value of less than 50 percent after three years. One way to research resale prices and depreciation of vehicles based on make, model, and year is by visiting many of the popular car-related Web sites featured in Chapter 7.

CAR SPEAK

REBATE—This is the amount by which a manufacturer reduces the price of a vehicle. Typically the buyer can apply a rebate to the cost of the vehicle or receive it in cash.

INCENTIVE—This is any of several means by which a manufacturer encourages the sales of specific vehicles. It could be a discount offered to a dealership or a cash refund or lower loan rate on a vehicle.

DEALER HOLDBACK—This is an allowance that a manufacturer provides to a dealer, usually two to three percent of the MSRP, often as a credit to the dealer's account. With a holdback, the dealer could pay the manufacturer less than the amount invoiced and then sell a vehicle at cost and still make a small profit. A dealer does not have to disclose to the buyer if there's a holdback.

INVOICE PRICE—This is what a dealer pays a manufacturer for a car, exclusive of holdbacks and other discounts. It's usually not what the vehicle actually costs the dealer.

Driving Smart

HIGHEST RESALE According to the editors of *Forbes* magazine (*www. forbesautos.com*), for the 2006 model year, these vehicles had the highest resale values based on 2006 base MSRP and residual values for 36-month projections for March through April 2006: Mini Cooper, Honda Accord, Toyota Avalon, Porsche 911 Carrera, Acura TL, Mercedes-Benz CL-Class, Honda Odyssey, Land Rover Range Rover Sport, Toyota Sequoia, and Toyota Tundra.

- **Size.** The interior dimensions are a measure of passenger comfort and stowage space. The exterior dimensions can be a measure of overall handling and maneuverability.

- **Test-Drive Experience.** You can get information online and in print, referrals from friends and relatives, and reviews by experts, but nothing replaces the need to test-drive a vehicle and evaluate the driving experience for yourself. During a test-drive, focus on things like functionality, comfort, luxury, quality of manufacturing, design, level of outside noise entering the passenger area, stability, smoothness of the ride, and anything else that's important to you.

- **Warranty.** All new vehicles come with a manufacturer's warranty that covers certain types of repairs for a specified number of years or a specified number of miles, whichever comes first. How long does the warranty last, relative to comparable vehicles? What does it cover? Is it comprehensive, bumper-to-bumper, or are there a lot of limitations? Will you have to pay a deductible for covered repairs? Be sure to read the fine print.

Driving Smart

GM WARRANTIES Starting with 2007 model year vehicles, GM began offering a five-year/100,000-mile warranty on all new passenger cars, light-duty trucks, and vans. This warranty features no deductible for all covered warrantable repairs required as a result of defects due to materials and/or quality of work for the power train components listed in the warranty (including engine, transmission, and drive systems).

PREP AND OTHER COSTS Look out for hidden costs and charges, such as dealer preparation fees, destination charges, extended warranty charges, and fees associated with accessories, and options (including installation). The salesperson should spell out all of these fees in the initial price quote and when you start negotiating and then not add any after you've negotiated your price and as you're moving forward with the purchase.

By evaluating each vehicle you're considering according to the criteria listed in this section, you'll be able to make a more intelligent decision. The more information you gather and the more relevant research you perform prior to your purchase, the better your chances of choosing a vehicle that'll provide the comfort, reliability, and functionality you want.

As you're reviewing all of the information you gather and comparing it with your test-driving experience, put all of the most important information into a context that's relevant to your wants and needs. For example, if a car can go from 0 mph to 60 mph in six seconds or less, that's impressive. However, if you generally drive slowly and you'll be using the car just around town, this feature isn't relevant to you.

What to Bring to the Dealership

When you begin visiting dealerships and looking at vehicles, you'll get a lot of information in a relatively short time. Keeping track of all this information, especially if you're not an expert on cars, will be a challenge.

To make the shopping and negotiating process easier, use this checklist to make sure you have everything you need when visiting dealerships:

❏ **Calculator.** Don't rely on the salesperson's math. Do your own calculations of the purchase price, the monthly payment, the effect of the interest rate and the size of the down payment on the monthly payment, etc.

❏ **Cell phone.** Being able to say, "I have to check with my spouse before making a decision" or "I want to call another dealership for a competitive quote before I commit" are two powerful tactics you can use in negotiating—if you have a cell phone.

❏ **Pen and paper.** Be prepared to take notes on each vehicle, the questions that come to you, and the answers you get.

❏ **Printouts** of your online research and pricing information. Don't rely on your memory. Have your information with you.

❏ **Your driver's license.** Without a valid driver's license, you won't be able to test-drive any vehicles.

Understanding How New Cars Are Priced

One of the most confusing things you're apt to encounter is all of the different prices quoted for the same new vehicle. With so much seemingly conflicting price information, it can become difficult to determine what a vehicle is actually worth, how much you should pay for it, and how much leeway you have to negotiate.

Understanding what each price means and how the prices are derived will help you negotiate the best price. The most important price information to know is what the dealer paid for the vehicle, how much other consumers have recently paid for an identical vehicle in your geographic area, and what rebates and incentives are currently in place that increase a dealer's profit. This information will give you negotiating power.

The following are descriptions of the various new car prices you'll encounter:

- **Base Price.** This is the suggested retail price of the vehicle, which should include all standard equipment and the factory warranty but will not include any added options or accessories. After you add the options you want, the price will probably be much higher.

- **Edmunds True Market Value.** Edmunds is an independent organization that publishes pricing information for all new vehicle makes and models. The company's pricing is based on extensive market research. According to the company, the Edmunds True Market Value (TMV) is a proprietary system for calculating what others are paying for new vehicles, based on sales data from geographic areas. When you request an Edmunds.com TMV report, you get a price estimate for the vehicle based on your ZIP code and the options you've chosen.

- **Invoice Price/Dealer Sticker Price.** This is what the manufacturer charges the dealership for the vehicle—in principle. Typically, the dealer pays less than the invoice price, because of rebates, discounts, allowances, and other types of incentives that dealers do not necessarily disclose to buyers. Determine if the invoice price includes the destination and delivery charge the dealership pays. If it's included, make sure you don't pay it twice, in the invoice and separately. To know what the dealerships are actually paying for vehicles (and determine how much profit they're making), you'll probably need to pay for car pricing information offered by Edmunds (*www.edmunds.com*), CarPrice.com (*www.carprice.com*), or Kelley Blue Book (*www.kbb.com*). This information is also published in car buying guides, *Consumer Reports,* and other publications available at your local bookstore or newsstand. When you begin negotiating, focus on the invoice price (or the price you know the dealer paid for the vehicle) and not on the manufacturer's suggested retail price (MSRP).

- **Kelley's New Car Blue Book Value.** This figure (available from *www.kbb.com* and from the company's printed directories) reflects a vehicle's actual selling price and is based on tens of thousands of recent sales transactions from auto dealers across the United States. According to the company, the New Car Blue Book Value is not based on a proprietary formula, but rather derived from actual new vehicle sales and extensive knowledge of the marketplace. Like the Edmunds True Market Value Price, you will have to research this pricing information on the Web. It will not be provided by the dealership.

- **Monroney Sticker Price/MSRP.** This is the price that by law must be displayed on a sticker on the vehicle's window. It lists the base price and the cost of each of the options installed by the manufacturer. It also lists the transportation and delivery charge. This same sticker will show the vehicle's fuel economy (mileage). Starting in September 2007, this sticker will also include vehicle safety information. The MSRP is the asking price for the vehicle; however, you can negotiate it down.

Negotiating Your Best Price

When negotiating the best price possible for a vehicle, the dealer's profit margin will partially affect the price you pay. The profit margin is the difference between what the dealer paid the manufacturer for the vehicle and what you pay for it. Rebates, incentives, and dealer holdbacks also affect your ability to negotiate, because they directly affect the dealer's profit margin. In addition to the profit on the vehicle, dealers also earn money when you add options and accessories, when they charge a preparation fee, when you purchase an extended warranty, and when you acquire financing through the dealership.

Driving Smart

NOT JUST THE INVOICE PRICE The dealer's invoice price may not be the only basis for calculating the profit margin. Often, there are factory-to-dealer incentives that enable the dealership to increase the profit, without the consumer necessarily knowing about it. Thus, if you know there are incentives in place, you can negotiate a price that's even lower than the invoice price. You can learn about factory-to-dealer incentives by doing research online. (See Chapter 7.) Don't rely on the dealership to tell you about them.

DEALER INCENTIVES Dealer incentives are programs the manufacturer uses to encourage dealers to sell slow-selling models or reduce inventories. These incentives are typically cash rebates or savings offered directly to the dealership, which the dealer may or may not pass along to the buyer. By doing research, you can learn about these incentives and take them into consideration when negotiating the price. When a dealer incentive is in place, it can increase the dealer's profit on the vehicle. Dealer incentives are not available for all makes and models of vehicles. They are usually offered at the end of a model year, just before and after manufacturers introduce the new line of vehicles for the upcoming year. They are also used when certain vehicles are not selling well enough.

REBATES TO YOU Sometimes manufacturers offer cash rebates and other incentives directly to buyers. In some cases, a cash rebate is offered only if you pay for the vehicle in cash, rather than financing it. Otherwise, a special financing deal may be offered, in the form of a lower interest rate. Sometimes, cash rebates are offered only to first-time buyers or loyal customers. Manufacturers offer rebates for various reasons and at certain times and often for specific makes and models only.

It's important to understand that, in addition to factory-to-dealer incentives, there may be consumer incentives from manufacturers (such as zero-percent financing or a cash-back allowance) that enable the consumer to save additional money on some new vehicles. Before starting to negotiate price, you should research the dealer invoice price of a vehicle, know what other consumers in your area have recently paid for that same vehicle, and determine what incentives are currently being offered. With this information, you'll be in a much better position to negotiate the best price from a dealership without a lot of haggling.

Again, before you start negotiating, work with the dealer to customize your vehicle with all of the options and accessories you want. (See Chapter 9.) Now, have the dealership come up with a starting price for that vehicle as equipped vehicle. Make sure that this price includes installation fees for all options and accessories and any license, title, destination, and prep fees.

Once you're given this asking price for the vehicle you want, exactly as you want it, start negotiating—without taking into consideration the trade-in value of your current vehicle (if you're trading in). After you have negotiated your best price and have reached an agreement, then start negotiating on the trade-in value. This should be a separate negotiation. Based on how much the dealership offers for your current vehicle and the research you've done to determine how much it's worth on the market, you can decide which makes more financial sense, to trade it in or to sell it privately.

Don't just focus on the monthly payment for your new vehicle, especially if you're financing it. Concentrate on negotiating the best possible purchase price. Then focus on finding the best financing option. The annual percentage rate (APR) determines how much the loan will cost you over time in interest. In addition to the APR (which will be based primarily on your credit score), also focus on the length of the loan.

Let's compare two loans, with different APRs and terms, so you can see how APRs and terms affect the monthly payment and the total cost of the loan. For this example, let's assume that the final negotiated price of the vehicle is $24,000. (To keep this simple, let's leave aside sales tax and any trade-in.)

The duration of a car loan can be 36 months, 48 months, 60 months, or even 72 months. It seldom makes sense to take on a car loan for 72 months, especially if there's a good chance you won't be driving that car in six years or the car is unlikely to last that long. (It's possible to refinance a car loan down the road, but you often won't receive the best rates. However, at some point you might consider consolidating your loan if you refinance your mortgage or take out a home equity loan, for example. Doing this could save you money in interest charges and offer tax advantages.)

Scenario 1

	36 Months (3 Years)	**60 Months (5 Years)**
Final Purchase Price	$24,000	$24,000
Amount Financed	$21,600	$21,600
10% Down Payment	$2,400	$2,400
APR	6%	6%
Monthly Payment	$657.11	$417.58
Total Price of Vehicle (including all interest, etc.)	$26,056	$27,455

Scenario 1 shows the difference in your monthly payment and total vehicle price if you had an above-average credit score and qualified for a loan with a 6 percent APR. (If your credit score is excellent, you could qualify for an even more competitive APR. At times, people with excellent credit are offered a 0 percent APR on financed vehicles.) It makes much more sense to finance a vehicle at 6 percent for three years and pay a total of $26,056 than it does to finance the vehicle for five years at 12 percent and pay $31,228. If you can afford the higher monthly payment, you'll save more down the road. Always consider the long term, the total payments, when evaluating your financing options.

Scenario 2

	36 Months (3 Years)	60 Months (5 Years)
Final Purchase Price	$24,000	$24,000
Amount Financed	$21,600	$21,600
10% Down Payment	$2,400	$2,400
APR	8%	8%
Monthly Payment	$676.86	$437.97
Total Price of Vehicle (including all interest, etc.)	$26,767	$28,678

In Scenario 2, at an 8 percent APR, if you obtained a three-year loan, your monthly payment would be $676.86 and you'd be spending $26,767 total. If you were to take this same loan for five years, your monthly payment would drop to $437.97, but you'd be $28,678 for the vehicle. That's $1,911 more in interest charges over the life of the loan.

Scenario 3

	36 Months (3 Years)	60 Months (5 Years)
Final Purchase Price	$24,000	$24,000
Amount Financed	$21,600	$21,600
10% Down Payment	$2,400	$2,400
APR	12%	12%
Monthly Payment	$717.42	$480.48
Total Price of Vehicle (including all interest, etc.)	$28,227	$31,228

In Scenario 3, let's assume your credit score is below average, so you'll need to pay a higher APR. (It should be noted that if your credit score is poor, you may also be required to pay more down.) In this scenario, if you took a loan for three years, your monthly payment would be $717.42. If that payment seems more than you can handle, you could borrow the same amount at the same rate for five years. Your monthly payment would be much lower, only $480.48, but you'd end up paying $31,229—$3,002 more.

This example shows how much more you'd pay in total if you took a loan for five years instead of three, to lower the monthly payment. It also shows how much more you'd pay if your credit were below average and the best APR you could get was 12 percent, in contrast with the 6 percent for which you could qualify if your credit was above average.

Playing with Numbers

If you're buying smart, it means playing with numbers—maybe lots of them. But you don't have to do all that math alone.

Take advantage of free, online car loan calculators to help determine what financing options make the most sense for you. You can quickly punch in a term and a rate and get the monthly car payment and the total price of the vehicle for each financing scenario. You can also determine if leasing a car would be smarter financially.

You can find a variety of auto-related finance calculators at these Web sites:

Yahoo! Autos: *autos.yahoo.com/finance/loan-calc/index.html*
Vehix.com: *www.vehix.com/finance/calculators/autoloan.aspx*
Cars.com: *www.cars.com/go/advice/financing/calc/loanCalc.jsp*
Bankrate.com: *www.bankrate.com/brm/rate/auto_home.asp*

Driving Smart

THE OTHER COSTS Figure out how much you can expect to pay for gas, maintenance, insurance, etc., based on your driving habits, geographic area, and personal situation. *Consumer Reports* magazine is one resource for researching the safety and the repair and maintenance costs of a particular make and model of vehicle. Another excellent resource is the U.S. Department of Transportation Auto Safety Hotline (800 424-9393), which provides information about recalls.

HOME EQUITY LOAN In addition to analyzing the various car financing options, if you're a homeowner, you might find it smarter financially to pay

---

for the vehicle using a home equity loan or a home equity line of credit or even by refinancing your mortgage. One reason for this is you could qualify for a better rate. Another reason is that, in most cases, these types of loans have tax advantages that car loans do not. Be sure to explore all of your options fully. An accountant or financial planner can help you determine if these financing alternatives would be better for you.

The Hidden Costs to Consider

In addition to the fees and charges directly associated with buying a vehicle, you may also be required to pay other fees, which could be added to the total cost after you've finished negotiating and before you sign the paperwork. Some of these fees and charges can be negotiated down, but some are mandatory and fixed.

Advertising Fees. This is an expense that most vehicle manufacturers automatically charge their dealerships, which then pass it along to consumers. If this charge is listed as part of the factory invoice price (dealer sticker price), it should not be added again as a separate charge. This fee is often negotiable and can sometimes be eliminated using the argument that advertising is part of the dealership's overhead and not your responsibility as a customer. The advertising fee can be between one and three percent of the base price.

Destination Charges (Freight). This is the cost of shipping the vehicle from the manufacturing facility to the dealership. It should already be included in the factory invoice price. Don't allow the dealer to add any additional destination charges beyond that. Also, this fee can sometimes be negotiated down or eliminated.

Excise Tax. This is a tax imposed by your state and/or (in many areas) local government, based on the value of the vehicle. It cannot be negotiated or eliminated. After you buy the vehicle and every year thereafter, you will receive a bill for this tax, which is separate from the sales tax you pay in buying the vehicle.

License and Title Fees. This is what the dealership pays to your state Department of Motor Vehicles or Registry of Motor Vehicles in order to register the vehicle and acquire license plates, a title, and registration in your name. The dealer adds these state fees to your bill and charges you a processing/handling fee. You can opt to handle this paperwork yourself to save a little money, but the time you save if the dealer handles this for you is well worth the typical processing/handling fee.

Dealer Preparation Fees. This is what some dealers charge for preparing the vehicle for sale once it arrives on their lot. This preparation consists basically of removing plastic from the seats, vacuuming, adding fluids, and putting on dealer decals. Read the sticker: in the price you may already be paying for "manufacturer's recommended pre-delivery service" or something similar. This charge can typically be negotiated down or eliminated.

Other Charges. Beware of charges like "additional dealer mark-up," "additional dealer profit," or "market value adjustment." These fees can typically be negotiated down or eliminated. These extra charges will be listed on the Monroney sticker and in your final paperwork at the time of purchase if they're applicable.

Sales Tax. This is the tax you pay to the state government based on the purchase price of the vehicle. You cannot negotiate the sales tax. However, if a neighboring state has a lower sales tax rate, you might be able to save money by traveling to that state and working with a dealership there to purchase your vehicle. (There may be state laws that make this a bad strategy. For example, your state may charge you a use tax or a sales tax.) Otherwise, plan to pay your state sales tax.

Driving Smart

SELLING PRIVATELY Sell your current vehicle privately instead of trading it in at the dealership. You'll almost always be able to get considerably more for it. However, if you're upside-down on a loan on your vehicle, trading it in may be the easiest option, unless you're willing to pay the amount outstanding on that loan and consider it an out-of-pocket expense.

LOW SCORE AND DEALER-ARRANGED LOANS Most car dealerships work with multiple lenders and can help their customers obtain a loan almost regardless of their credit scores. But if your credit score is below average the deal you're offered won't necessarily be competitive. To keep the monthly payment reasonable, the lender may extend the loan to 60 months (five years), for example.

There are two problems with this. First, you end up paying more. Second, if the vehicle will last only three to four years, you could wind up upside-down on the loan when you attempt to sell the car. This means that you owe more on the car than it's worth as a trade-in or in a sale. So, for example, if you still owe $10,000 on the car, but the most you could get selling it is only $8,500, you'd still have to pay $1,500 out-of-pocket to rid yourself of the car.

If finances are tight, find a car that you expect to last you three to five years and then don't accept a car loan with a term beyond the time you anticipate owning that car. If possible, go for three years, not five. Not only will this save you money in interest, you will own the car outright much sooner and avoid going upside-down.

Completing a Car Loan Application

When completing a credit/financing application at a dealership, you'll be required to provide personal and financial information, including the following:

- Your full name
- Current address and phone number (plus old addresses if you've moved within the past three years)
- A copy of your driver's license
- Your Social Security number
- Your date of birth
- Three years worth of employment history
- Your occupation
- Your income

- Details about checking and savings accounts
- Permission for the dealership or lender to access your credit report(s) and credit score

When financing a vehicle, the purchase price and the terms of the financing should be two totally separate negotiations, even though you may be dealing with the same person at the dealership. First, negotiate the price. Next, negotiate the value of your trade-in (if any). Finally, negotiate the financing. Don't allow the salesperson or dealership's financing manager to offer you a deal just based on the monthly payment. Calculate the true (total) price of the car, including what you'll be paying in interest.

The rate of the financing your dealer offers may be higher than the rate you could get for similar financing from a bank or credit union. Your dealer will typically not tell you that you could qualify for a better rate elsewhere. Remember: you are expected to negotiate!

Buying a Used Car Can Save You Big Bucks

If you have the money, buying a new car is a viable option. However, if you want to get the most car possible for the money you have to spend, buying a used (pre-owned) car may be a smarter financial decision. The pros and cons of buying a used car are discussed in the next chapter.

Buying a Used Car

WHAT'S IN THIS CHAPTER

- The steps in buying a used vehicle
- Pitfalls
- Finding a used vehicle
- Buying from a private seller
- Working with a used car dealership
- Negotiating your best price

B uying a used, pre-owned, or certified pre-owned (CPO) vehicle is very much like buying a new vehicle. The big difference is that you'll need to do more research about each specific vehicle you're considering in order to get the most reliable one.

What You Need to Know About Used Cars

The first part of the additional research on any used vehicle is to get the vehicle identification number (VIN) and then use it to obtain a detailed vehicle history report. Vehicle history reports can be ordered online. The first company to offer this service was CARFAX, which accesses 4,400 information sources and a database of more than two billion records to compile reports that are e-mailed almost immediately to customers. CARFAX—*www.carfax.com*—offers two options: a single report and an unlimited number of reports for one month. With the second option, customers also get a *CARFAX Safety & Reliability Report* that includes information about the make and model. *Consumer Guide* also provides vehicle history reports, at *www.autocheck.com*. The company draws vehicle history information from the Experian database (with 1.7 billion records) and uses its own repair information.

The biggest potential drawback to buying a used vehicle is that you don't know how that vehicle was treated. Without doing research, you also don't know if the odometer has been tampered with, if the vehicle has been involved in any major accidents, and if any components of the vehicle are likely to need significant and costly repairs in the near future. It's crucial to know what repairs (routine or otherwise) lie ahead, especially if you're buying a used vehicle "as is"—with no warranty.

CAR SPEAK

AS IS—This means simply that, whatever the condition of the vehicle, the buyer is assuming total responsibility for it and for any repairs. No warranty or guarantee is offered by the seller, whether manufacturer, dealership, or private seller. Vehicles offered "as is" tend to be cheaper, but offer the least peace of mind for the buyer. Another term for "as is" used by dealers is "with all faults." In certain states, if a car is sold "as is," any implied warranties that may otherwise be enforceable do not apply. In other words, you're not protected by any "lemon laws."

LEMON LAW—This is a colloquial term for any law that establishes standards of quality and performance for motor vehicles. There is a federal law—the Magnuson-Moss Warranty Act—and every state has a law. The state lemon laws differ from state to state. Not all state laws cover used or leased vehicles.

Driving Smart

INSPECT BEFORE YOU BUY Whether you're buying a used vehicle from a dealership or a private seller, at auction, or through some other method, you'll want to pay a mechanic to inspect the vehicle carefully before you buy it. You'll also want to obtain a vehicle history report and test-drive the vehicle.

Another important consideration when purchasing a used vehicle is the warranty (if any). Are you able to take advantage of whatever remains of the manufacturer's warranty? If so, for how much time or how many miles? If the original warranty has expired or is no longer valid, who is providing the new warranty (or extended warranty)? Is this something the dealership, the manufacturer, or a third party is offering? How much extra will the warranty cost you? What exactly is covered and for how long? These are all important questions that'll help you avoid having to pay for costly repairs on your used vehicle.

Some of the benefits to buying a used vehicle were discussed in Chapter 3. Perhaps the biggest benefit if your budget is limited is you get much more for your money buying used than buying new. If the used vehicle is between one and three years old, it has already depreciated in value. If, however, it is well-made, it should still have plenty of reliable life left in it.

It's definitely not uncommon for a quality vehicle from some manufacturers to last for 100,000 or even 200,000 miles or more miles without requiring significant repairs. However, to achieve this, the vehicle must be maintained well. If you're acquiring a vehicle that has been abused or neglected by the previous owner(s) or that has already experienced problems, you could be inheriting those problems and a pile of future repair bills if you're not careful.

Another problem you could encounter when shopping for a used vehicle is car salespeople or dealerships that are less than trustworthy or even downright dishonest. It's important to find a dealership you can trust. If you're buying from a private seller, you should be able to get a sense of that person's honesty as the two of you talk about his or her vehicle.

This chapter explores what you need to know in order to make an intelligent decision when buying a used (pre-owned) or CPO vehicle. (Additional information about CPOs and their benefits can be found in Chapter 3.)

Driving Smart

TRUST BUT VERIFY Never rely on the seller's word about the history of the vehicle, how well it was maintained, or its current condition.

NO THREE-DAY GRACE PERIOD Contrary to popular belief, a dealership is not required to offer a three-day right to cancel to used car buyers. In other words, once you purchase the vehicle, it's yours to keep, typically with no refunds or exchanges possible. In some cases, a dealer will offer a money-back guarantee, a "cooling off period," or a "no-questions-asked return policy." However, unless an offer like this is specifically spelled out in writing by the dealership, it does not exist. Thus, it's essential that you make intelligent decisions.

How Used Vehicles Are Priced

The price of a used vehicle is determined by a variety of factors. Through research on popular car-related Web sites and/or published pricing guides, you can easily obtain information about what specific vehicles are worth, based on the following criteria:

- Depreciation
- Make, model, and year
- Mileage
- Overall condition
- Optional features and accessories
- Warranty

Driving Smart

INDEPENDENT EXPERTISE Take advantage of independent pricing sources for used cars, such as Kelley Blue Book (*www.kbb.com*), Edmunds (*www.edmunds.com*), TraderOnline (*www.traderonline.com*), Autoweb (*www.autoweb.com*), Consumer Reports (*www.consumerreports.org*), and the National Automobile Dealers Association Official Used Car Guide (*www.nadaguides.com*). Chapter 7 lists these and other Web sites to guide you.

It's important to understand that the asking price for a used car, no matter who is selling it, is rarely set in stone. In other words, if you want to get the best deal, plan on negotiating. One thing you have working in your favor is that you have an incredibly large selection of used cars to choose from, so finding the exact vehicle you want is easy—especially if you're using the Internet in your search.

If you begin negotiating for a vehicle, but the seller is unwilling to accept your offer, you can always walk away and typically find a handful of comparable used vehicles in a matter of minutes and probably more motivated sellers. In many cases, private sellers are eager to sell their vehicles as quickly as possible for prices that are higher than what dealerships would pay for them as trade-ins. Since a dealership will typically offer a very low price (often five percent less than the vehicle's wholesale value), you can offer a little more to the seller and still get an excellent deal.

Used Car Lingo

An ad can tell you a lot about a vehicle that's for sale. However, what's stated in the ad is determined by the seller. Some sellers try to make their used vehicles sound more appealing. As a general rule, ads that sound too good to be true typically are. Thus, if you see a used vehicle you know is worth $10,000 selling for only $4,500, chances are it has serious problems.

The following are some of the words and abbreviations commonly found in ads for used cars.

- **2-DR/3-DR/4-DR/5-DR**—Two-door, three-door hatchback, four-door, five-door hatchback
- **5SP**—Manual five-speed transmission
- **A/C**—Air-conditioned
- **Asking Price**—The price the seller would like to receive for the vehicle, typically a starting point for a negotiation
- **Auto or AT**—Automatic transmission
- **Best Offer or B/O**—Typically an indication the buyer is eager to sell quickly and extremely willing to negotiate, sometimes after an asking price, as "or best offer" or "OBO"

- **Cherry Condition**—In excellent condition, a term typically used for a classic or collectible vehicle
- **Clean**—Generally, detailed professionally or otherwise refurbished
- **CPO**—Certified pre-owned (completely refurbished and detailed by professionals to meet the manufacturer's standards for a new vehicle)
- **Excellent Condition**—Fully operational and well maintained, both mechanics and appearances
- **Firm**—Typically means the seller is unwilling to negotiate on the price
- **FWD/RWD/4WD**—Front-wheel drive, rear-wheel drive, four-wheel drive
- **Good Condition or G/C**—Typically operational, but with minor problems, either mechanically or in appearances
- **Lemon**—With a history of potentially serious mechanical problems ... and not worth even considering, no matter how low the price
- **Like-New**—A term used to describe virtually all CPO vehicles (which means also with a manufacturer's warranty) and any vehicle that looks and drives as if it were new.
- **Loaded**—With lots of options and accessories, which generally raise the price, whether you actually want them or not
- **Mint Condition**—Same as "excellent" or even "like-new," a term typically used for a classic or collectible vehicle

- **mpg**—Miles per gallon
- **Needs Work**—Requiring potentially major and costly repairs to get into full working condition: warning lights and sirens should go off in your head
- **Negotiable**—The seller is very motivated to sell, although not necessarily to you, so know what the vehicle is worth and negotiate fairly
- **OK**—Typically, "so-so" or "not great," especially for the overall condition, so expect problems
- **P/L** – Power locks
- **P/W** – Power windows

The Steps in Buying a Used Vehicle

While the experience of buying a used vehicle will be different for every buyer, these are the primary steps in this process:

1. **Do your research.** Use the Internet, read car magazines for reviews, and attend car shows, for example, to learn about pricing, to find out what's available, to obtain information about vehicle safety and consumer satisfaction records, and to better define your needs.

2. **Determine what you can afford.** Evaluate your overall budget (income, current living expenses, and debts) so you know how much you can actually afford, not how much your credit reports and credit score indicate you could finance.

3. **Select a specific make and model.** There are thousands of makes and models of used cars on the market. Narrow

down your choices according to your wants and needs, to a handful of comparable vehicles. Start by choosing a vehicle category, such as an SUV or four-door sedan, and then decide which makes and models you can afford. You can do this by checking popular car-related Web sites or by reading reviews. As you're narrowing down your choices, do more research about each vehicle (make, model, and year). Keep in mind a make and model might vary considerably from model year to model year in terms of design, quality, price, and features.

4. **Research the worth of each vehicle on your list.** Use resources such as Kelley Blue Book or Edmunds to determine the value of the vehicle based on its make, model, year, mileage, condition, and your geographic area. Regardless of the asking price, prices of used vehicles are almost always negotiable. (If a price is not negotiable, the ad will typically qualify the asking price as "firm.")

Driving Smart

CHECK THE INSURANCE COST Once you know the make, model, and year you want, you can determine how much it'll cost to insure that vehicle by contacting your insurance company. (This is information you'll need when setting your budget.)

5. **Shop around for the best price.** After researching and narrowing down your ideal choice to a specific make, model, and year and deciding on the configuration you want, start

shopping around for the best price for that specific vehicle. Contact dealers and/or private sellers.

6. **Obtain a detailed vehicle history report.** Do not rely on information from the seller or take the seller's word about a vehicle's history. In addition to obtaining your own CARFAX report, for example, request copies of the vehicle's maintenance records (from the owner or seller or from any garage that has done work on the vehicle).

Driving Smart

LEARN THE TERMS To better understand the CARFAX report you acquire from *www.carfax.com*, access and read the detailed glossary on the Web site, at *www.carfax.com/definitions/glossary.cfm*.

7. **Test-drive the vehicle and inspect it closely.** By test-driving a vehicle, even if you're not a mechanic, you can probably determine if there is anything significantly wrong with it. Be alert for strange noises, smells, and leaks and pay attention to how the vehicle performs. Be sure to drive on side streets, flat roads, hills (at slow and normal speeds), and a highway (at a steady speed of 55 to 65 mph, depending on the posted speed limit).

Driving Smart

TAKE A FRIEND ALONG For your own safety, before agreeing to meet a private seller to test-drive a vehicle, confirm his or her identity and take along a friend or a relative. Meet in a public place and during daylight hours.

Driving Smart

HIGH MILEAGE QUESTIONS The average driver will put about 15,000 miles per year on a vehicle. So, under normal use, a three-year-old vehicle should have around 45,000 miles on the odometer. If the mileage on the vehicle you're looking at is significantly higher, ask why. A vehicle with more miles will have experienced more wear.

8. **Ask the seller questions about the vehicle.** The more you can learn about the vehicle from the seller, the more intelligent you can be in making your decision about it. The following are some preliminary questions to ask on the phone or in person:

- Why are you selling the vehicle?
- How many miles are on the odometer?
- What is the condition of the vehicle?
- How well equipped is the vehicle?
- Are you the original owner?
- Has the vehicle ever been involved in a major accident?
- Do you have copies of the vehicle's service records and receipts?
- How much are you asking for the vehicle? Are you flexible on the price?
- What color is the car? Is it the original paint job?
- What major repairs have been done on the car?
- How has the car been maintained? Have you done all of the recommended maintenance?

- Does the car have any rust?
- What repair work still needs to be done on the car?
- How reliable is the car in cold weather? Has it ever broken down?

Driving Smart

USE THE PHONE You'll save a lot of time and trouble by interviewing a seller on the phone, before meeting in person to test-drive the vehicle. Ask questions to determine if the vehicle will meet the specifications you're looking for. Asking the right questions in advance can help you eliminate unsuitable cars quickly.

9. **Have an independent mechanic inspect the vehicle.** If you're still interested in purchasing a vehicle after test-driving it, hire an independent mechanic to inspect it. It will be an out-of-pocket expense, but it's a good investment. If you determine the vehicle needs repairs, you can use this knowledge to negotiate a better price or you can decide to continue your search. Hiring a mechanic to inspect a vehicle should cost no more than $100 and take about one hour.

10. **Review the warranty (if any).** When you're purchasing a used vehicle, a warranty will give you peace of mind and help cover costly repairs if necessary. If no warranty is offered, look into purchasing an optional (but often costly) extended warranty, from the dealer, the manufacturer, or a third party. Determine what the warranty covers, for how long, and if there are any deductibles.

11. **Start negotiating.** Through online research, you can determine what others in your area have paid for the same vehicle. If you're not doing well enough with one dealer or private seller, try another. You may have to negotiate with several to get a good price.

12. **Negotiate your trade-in.** If you'll be trading in your vehicle at a dealership, work at getting the best possible price. You'd probably get a higher price if you sold it privately. Doing this takes more time and effort, however.

13. **Apply for financing.** Whether you're getting financing through a bank, a credit union, or another lender, find the best rate for which you qualify and the lowest fees. Most lenders charge slightly higher interest rates on loans for used vehicles than for new vehicles. However, if your credit is below average, many used car dealers will be more aggressive than new car dealers to get your loan application approved. The financing deal you're offered, however, may not be great.

14. **Complete the paperwork.** There's a lot of paperwork involved in buying a used car. Make sure that you have plenty of time, so you can read it all and get answers to all of your questions. Whatever you sign will become legally binding. All oral agreements—whether about the vehicle, the terms of the sale, or the financing—should be put in writing. Most dealers offer to acquire the title, license, registration, and inspection sticker on your behalf (for a fee). This will save you a lot of time and trouble.

Driving Smart

CHECK THE TITLE Check the validity of the vehicle's title, especially if you're purchasing it from a private seller. Make sure the vehicle is not stolen and that you're buying it from the actual (legal) owner. You can research a vehicle's owner using the vehicle registration number and/or the vehicle's registration or license plate number. The name on the title and registration should be identical to the name of the seller you're working with.

15. **Obtain insurance.** Shop around for appropriate coverage and the best price. (Chapter 10 covers automotive insurance.)

Driving Smart

NO GOING BACK Once all of the paperwork is signed, the vehicle becomes yours legally. You generally won't be able to return the vehicle if you experience buyer's remorse or change your mind, for whatever reason.

SOLVE PROBLEMS FIRST Before taking possession of the vehicle, inspect the exterior and interior thoroughly. Take the vehicle for a test-drive. If there's a problem, bring it to the attention of the salesperson or the seller immediately. Do not take possession of the vehicle until the situation is resolved to your satisfaction.

Pitfalls in Buying a Used Vehicle

Any car dealer who sells more than five used vehicles in a 12-month period must comply with the Federal Trade Commission's Used Car Rule (except in Maine and Wisconsin, which are exempt because both states have similar regulations). One of the requirements of that rule is that a dealer must post a Buyers Guide before offering a used vehicle for sale. This two-page guide must tell you, in writing, whether the vehicle comes with a warranty (and if so, what type of warranty) or if it's being sold "as is." If any type of warranty is being offered, the Guide must indicate what percentage of the repair costs will be covered under that warranty and what deductibles will apply for the owner.

One of the biggest pitfalls for used car shoppers is that they rely on verbal promises by the seller. In reality, unless what is promised is put in writing, it is not typically binding or enforceable. Thus, the verbal promise means absolutely nothing. Many used car salespeople will tell you whatever they think you want to hear in order to make the sale. (Of course, there are also some extremely honest used car salespeople and dealerships out there.)

IMPLIED WARRANTY—This is an obligation under state laws **CAR SPEAK** for dealers to ensure that the vehicles they sell meet reasonable quality standards. In some states, any used vehicle sold by a dealer comes with an implied warranty, whether or not a formal written warranty is provided. However, in most states dealers can use the words "as is" or "with all faults" in a written notice to buyers to eliminate implied warranties. There is no specified time period for implied warranties.

To avoid problems down the road, avoid buying a used vehicle that has been in a major accident, that is possibly stolen, that has been previously salvaged, that's been classified as a lemon, or that has an extremely high number of miles on the odometer. Also, if the car is more than a few years old and comes with no warranty, check the vehicle's maintenance history so you can determine if it's already received expensive maintenance, like changing the timing belt. In this situation, hiring an independent mechanic to do a thorough inspection can be extremely beneficial. Otherwise, you could get stuck with a vehicle that requires thousands of dollars of repairs in the near future.

Driving Smart

KNOW WHERE THE SELLER IS If you're purchasing from a private seller, be sure to obtain the seller's address and phone number and whatever other information might help you track him or her down later, if necessary. You may discover you've been misled and the vehicle has serious problems that the seller failed to disclose. The contract you sign when purchasing the vehicle may not allow you any recourse.

WOULD YOU BUY A USED CAR FROM ...? Before doing business with a used car dealer, especially an independent, check out the dealership. One way to do this is by contacting the local Better Business Bureau (*www.bbb.org*). Ideally, if you can find a used car dealer through a referral from a satisfied customer, you have a much better chance of being happy with your experience.

Major Problems in Used Vehicles

The following is a list of potential problem areas to check when evaluating and test-driving a used vehicle:

- Air conditioner/heater

- Brake system
- Cooling system
- Dashboard gauges and warning devices
- Differential
- Electrical system
- Engine
- Exhaust system
- Exterior (rust, dents, scratches, holes, marred paint)
- Frame and body
- Fuel system
- Steering system
- Suspension system
- Tires
- Transmission and driveshaft
- Wheels

Driving Smart

CHECK THE ACCESSORIES Check that all accessories and options are fully operational, such as the GPS and the audio system (CD player, AM/FM radio, etc.).

USE ALL YOUR SENSES During the test-drive, look, listen, and smell for signs of problems. After a test-drive, check the vehicle for leaks, strange odors, or smoke.

Finding a Used Vehicle

Once you know the make and model of vehicle you want and have decided how old it can be and how much mileage it can have, the best places to start searching for a used vehicle are online and in your local newspaper. Because you'll have so many options, you can decide whether you're more comfortable working with private sellers, independent used car dealerships, or authorized new car dealerships that also sell used vehicles.

There are many terms associated with used vehicles that help to differentiate among them and that could enable the seller to ask for more money for that vehicle.

A *demonstrator* is a vehicle that has never been owned, leased, or used as a rental. It has very low mileage. It could have been used for test-drives and/or driven by the dealer's staff. These cars are not considered new, but because the mileage is very low they still come with the full manufacturer's warranty and are typically in "like-new" condition. Demonstrators can be purchased for a little less than new vehicles.

A *program car* is a vehicle that may be relatively new (less than two or three years old) and have relatively low mileage, but was used as a short-term lease vehicle, for example. Thus, it may have been driven by many people, who may or may not have maintained it properly.

Driving Smart

STILL IN BUSINESS? When shopping for a used car, avoid makes and models that are no longer being produced or whose manufacturer is no longer in business. Getting parts and service for such vehicles is extremely difficult and often costly. But this may be acceptable if the vehicle is vintage, classic, and/or collectible.

A *fleet car* is a vehicle that was part of group of vehicles owned by a company and driven by employees. These are vehicles that could have been abused by their drivers and have excessive wear. Former rental cars also fall into this category.

Working with a Used Car Dealership

While new cars are typically sold by authorized dealerships that represent specific manufacturers, used cars can also be sold by independent dealerships, rental car companies, leasing companies, and used car superstores, as well as by private sellers. It's even possible to purchase a used vehicle on the Internet—but if you do this you should definitely check the vehicle out in person and take it for a test-drive before making the purchase.

The dealership you visit may offer "no-haggle" prices, which means that the sticker price on the vehicle is the selling price—period. In many situations, however, you are expected to negotiate the price.

Driving Smart

AUCTIONS: BE CAUTIOUS Auctions can offer incredible, money-saving opportunities for a used car buyer. However, most auctions don't allow test-drives of the vehicles. Also, it's often difficult to acquire details about a vehicle before the bidding. If you opt to purchase a vehicle at auction, proceed with caution and make sure you fully understand what you'd be getting, before you bid. Auction sales are final. This is not an ideal option for most car shoppers.

You may also encounter factory-certified pre-owned vehicles, which, as you learned in Chapter 3, are vehicles that have been fully refurbished and transformed into "like-new" condition by factory-authorized mechanics or dealerships.

What's Next?

Now that you know what's involved with buying a car, either new or used, let's consider another option—leasing. That's what the next chapter covers.

If, however, you're set on buying, check out Chapter 7 for details about some extremely useful Web sites and online services that can make researching and shopping much faster, easier, and more effective.

CHAPTER 6

The Commonsense
Approach to Leasing a Car

WHAT'S IN THIS CHAPTER

- The difference between buying and leasing
- The pros and cons of leasing
- Deciding if leasing is right for you
- Potential pitfalls of leasing

For some people (but not all), leasing is a smart alternative to purchasing a vehicle. The concept of leasing equipment or real estate has been prevalent in the corporate world for decades. However, it wasn't until the late 1980s that *vehicle leases* became popular among consumers.

A few years ago, when zero-percent interest on auto financing was being offered widely, leasing temporarily became less popular. Today, however, with the rising cost of new vehicles and interest rates for auto loans also on the rise, leasing is again becoming more popular. As of 2006, research shows that one out of five new cars is being leased rather than purchased.

CAR SPEAK   **VEHICLE LEASE**—This is a legal agreement between the *lessor* and the *lessee* about the use of a vehicle. A lease is documented by a contract that specifies the terms and limitations of that use, the length of the agreement, and the monthly payment for use of that vehicle. A typical vehicle lease can last for 24, 36, 48, or 60 months.

LESSOR—This is the company that allows use of a vehicle to a *lessee* through a lease.

LESSEE—This is the party that acquires use of a vehicle from a *lessor* through a lease.

The monthly payments for leasing a vehicle are always lower than for buying that same vehicle. However, there are limitations, specific terms, and costs associated with a lease that make this option less appealing to some people—especially consumers with less than stellar credit or without a stable income to support monthly payments for two to five years.

While the concept of leasing is relatively straightforward, the actual process of leasing a vehicle is not so straightforward, involving mathematical calculations to figure out the monthly payment. Also, most car dealerships simply act as outside agents for leasing companies and may not be able to accurately and adequately explain all of the terms of a lease agreement. For a detailed glossary of the many terms associated with leasing, visit *www.pueblo.gsa.gov/cic_text/cars/key2leas/ glossary.htm*.

Driving Smart

LEASE USED Leasing a vehicle rather than purchasing has become a popular option among consumers. It's also possible to lease a used vehicle, which, as you'd expect, can be a much more affordable option. Used car leases are available from some dealerships, although they're less common than new car leases.

How Vehicle Leases Work

When you purchase a new vehicle, you're paying its value to acquire full ownership. When you lease a vehicle, however, you're paying only for the depreciation on that vehicle while you're driving it. This depreciation represents the difference in value between the purchase (new) price of the vehicle (the *capitalized cost* or *cap cost*) and the vehicle's value at the end of the lease term (the *residual value*). The amount of your monthly payment when you lease a vehicle will be calculated primarily based on the projected residual value of the vehicle at the end of your lease. This amount is amortized over the length of the lease and divided into equal monthly payments.

CAR SPEAK **CAPITALIZED COST (CAP COST)**—This is the negotiated total price of a new vehicle being leased. It's comparable to the negotiated price of a new vehicle being purchased.

RESIDUAL VALUE—This is the worth of a vehicle at a given time, the difference between the purchase price and the amount of *depreciation*. In a vehicle lease, this value is estimated at the beginning of the lease and used as the basis for calculating the monthly payments. The actual value of the vehicle at the end of the lease period could be significantly higher or lower.

Your monthly payment on a vehicle lease will also be determined by the lease interest rate. This is a monthly finance charge imposed by the leasing company. At the time that you sign the lease, the lease inception, you'll be expected to make a payment. The amount is calculated by adding up your down payment, the acquisition fee (administrative costs), the state sales/use taxes, a security deposit (refundable), a dealer preparation fee, licensing fees, a lease-end disposition fee (maybe), and the first month's payment. This lease inception payment and how it was calculated will be printed in the lease agreement.

CAR SPEAK **DISPOSITION FEE**—This is a fee often charged by a lessor to cover the costs of preparing and selling the lease vehicle at the end of the lease. Also known as a *disposal fee* and a *termination fee*.

Buy or Lease a Car Without Getting Taken for a Ride

While the formula for calculating a monthly lease payment is somewhat complex, the concept behind the formula is straightforward. You start with the initial price of the car, say $25,000, and a lease term, say 36 months. The leasing company determines that after three years the residual value of the car will be $13,000. This means that during the lease the value of the vehicle is expected to drop by $12,000. That's what you must pay for use of the lease vehicle for three years. Now, divide the $12,000 by 36. The monthly payment based on this formula is about $333.33. That's simple enough. However, you also need to add other costs and fees associated with leasing, including the *money factor* and the sales tax, for example, in order to calculate the monthly payment.

MONEY FACTOR—This is a figure that represents the interest rate **CAR SPEAK** charged for a lease, used in calculating the monthly payments. The money factor is the interest rate percentage divided by 2,400. (In this formula, 2,400 is always used, regardless of the length of the loan.) For example, an interest rate of 7 percent expressed as a money factor is .0029. (To convert a money factor to an interest rate, APR, multiply by 2,400. For example, a money factor of .0035 would be an interest rate of 8.4 percent.) Dealers will sometimes quote a money factor as a larger decimal (multiplied by 100), because a money factor of 2.97, for example, sounds better than .00297. Also called a *lease factor*, a *lease fee*, or simply a *factor*.

The following is an example of a lease calculation. Once you've collected the pertinent information, it's easier to figure out the best financing deal if you use an online calculator.

Sample Lease Calculation
Information

Vehicle MSRP:	$27,000
Capitalization Cost:	$25,000 (negotiated price of the vehicle)
Down Payment:	$500
Additional Costs:	$500 (acquisition fee, luxury tax, extended warranty, etc.)
Cap Cost Reductions:	$500 (down payment)
Local Sales Tax:	6.25%
Money Factor:	.0029 (equivalent to 6.96% APR)
Lease Term:	36 months
Residual Value:	$14,000

Results (Using Online Calculator)

Monthly Lease Payment:	$419.44 + $26.22 tax = $445.66
Depreciation:	$11,000
Finance Charge:	$4,100
Total Sales Tax:	$975
Total Payments:	$16,044
Total Lease Cost:	$16,575.25

You are responsible for all taxes, fees, maintenance costs, and insurance associated with the vehicle during the time you have possession of it. You'll also be charged for any damage to the vehicle and any excessive mileage. These fees and the terms and conditions of the lease will all be defined, in writing, within the lease agreement. This is a legally binding document. Upon signing it, you will be bound by all of its terms, so it's essential that you understand what it says and what it means.

When you sign a lease, the information in it will be posted on your credit report with one, two, or all three major credit bureaus. The lease will appear on your credit report in the same way as a loan. And, just as with a loan, if you make the monthly payments on time you improve your credit score, but if you making the payments late you will damage your credit score.

As you know, all vehicles are not created equal. Some vehicles maintain their value over time better than others. For example, companies like Honda, Toyota, Volkswagen, and Mercedes-Benz have reputations for manufacturing quality vehicles that retain more of their value over time. Because you're basically paying for depreciation, a vehicle with an excellent residual value will make leasing more economically viable.

The longer the lease term, the greater the depreciation and the lower the residual value of the vehicle. The LeaseGuide. com Web site reports that the best cars to lease are those with a 24-month residual value of at least 50 percent of their MSRP value. You can determine the residual value of specific new vehicles, based on make, model, and year, through research online.

A typical vehicle lease is between 24 months and 48 months. To avoid getting stuck with repair bills, never sign a lease that extends past the term of the manufacturer's warranty and try to select a vehicle that offers a bumper-to-bumper warranty with no deductibles.

Negotiate your best price for the lease; the price of the vehicle (the capitalization cost) is where you can negotiate the most. The other terms of the lease—such as the residual value, the down payment, the security deposit, and the acquisition fee—are often non-negotiable or at least harder to negotiate, unless you're working directly with the leasing company (rather than a dealership acting as a representative of the leasing company). Remember: while it's often easier to work with a dealership to set up a lease, you can always seek out a leasing deal elsewhere—from banks, credit unions, and independent leasing companies, for example—and perhaps get better terms and rates.

Driving Smart

USE AN ONLINE CALCULATOR Lease payments are always going to be lower than if you were to finance the purchase of the same vehicle. To help determine what your monthly lease payments will be, use a Basic Lease Calculator, like the one found online at the LeaseGuide.com Web site (*www.leaseguide.com/calc.htm*). However, lower monthly payments do not make leasing the ideal option for everyone.

LOWER THE CAPITALIZATION When working with a dealership, always negotiate the lowest possible capitalization cost (purchase price) for the lease vehicle. This will lower your monthly payment. The capitalization cost you negotiate should include certain fees, such as the acquisition fee and any available rebates and other incentives.

CLOSED-END LEASE–A vehicle lease that ends at the conclu- **CAR SPEAK**
sion of the term: the lessee returns the vehicle and has no further responsibilities (other than to pay for any excessive
mileage or repair work). In a closed-end lease, the lessor must
predict the residual value of the vehicle. This type of lease is generally more
suitable for the average person. Closed-end lease payments are somewhat
higher than open-end lease payments. Also known as a *walk-away lease*.

OPEN-END LEASE–A vehicle lease that requires the lessee at the conclusion of the term to pay any difference between the residual value of the
vehicle and the market value. An open-end lease allows unlimited mileage.
This type of lease is used primarily for commercial purposes; it is typically
not suitable for personal use. Also known as a *finance lease*.

The Potential Benefits of Leasing

Leasing a vehicle offers several benefits. The down payment
for leasing a vehicle is typically lower than for purchasing the
same vehicle. The monthly payment is also typically 30 to 60
percent lower for lease than for purchasing. Because the costs
are lower, people who lease are able to afford nicer, more luxurious vehicles than they could afford to buy. They're also
able to upgrade to a new car more often. People who lease are
also responsible for fewer maintenance expenses. In addition,
they may qualify for tax benefits, especially if they use the
vehicle for business purposes. At the end of the lease, they
simply return the vehicle; they save the time and effort of selling or trading in. The lessee has no ownership of the vehicle
at any time. (It should be noted that a lease is unlike a rental

in some key respects. For example, if you lease a vehicle, any licensed driver who has insurance is allowed to drive the vehicle while it's in your possession.)

Driving Smart

RECOMMENDED SITE LeaseGuide.com (*www.leaseguide.com*) offers information on leasing a vehicle and useful tools. The online Lease Calculator, for example, will help you determine if leasing a vehicle makes financial sense. An exclusive interview with Al Hearn, a leading expert on vehicle leasing and founder of Leaseguide.com, is featured later in this chapter.

Another benefit of leasing is that there are no excise taxes to pay, since you don't actually own the vehicle; you'll pay only a sales tax, which is distributed throughout the term of the lease as part of the monthly payment. This can save you several hundred dollars per year. If you're using the leased vehicle for business purposes, consult your accountant about tax benefits.

The Potential Disadvantages of Leasing

Leasing is totally different from renting. You can go to your local Hertz, Avis, or Enterprise rental office and rent a vehicle for a day, a week, or a month. With a lease, the term is typically 24, 36, 48, or even 60 months. When you rent a vehicle, you can return it at any time and pay only for the time for which you had possession of the vehicle. With a lease, typically you cannot return or exchange the vehicle until the lease term ends. (In some cases, you can get out of a lease, but there's typically a hefty penalty to do so.)

Driving Smart

WHO SHOULD LEASE Leasing is most suitable for people with a stable and regular income who will be able to make their ongoing monthly payments on time for the entire term of the lease. If you terminate the lease, for whatever reason, you'll be responsible for paying an early termination fee, plus all remaining monthly payments, regardless of whether you continue to drive the vehicle or not. If you don't think you'll be able to make the monthly payments, don't lease a vehicle.

THEY'RE BINDING Lease agreements are binding and involve financial responsibilities just like a mortgage or a loan. If you experience medical problems or if you die, you or your heirs will still be responsible for making the monthly lease payments. So, if you're concerned about your health during the next three to five years, don't consider leasing.

There's another important difference between renting and leasing. When you rent a vehicle, your agreement typically allows you to drive an unlimited number of miles, with no additional fees. When you lease, however, you're given a mileage allowance that is typically between 10,000 and 15,000 miles per year. If you drive more miles than allowed in the lease agreement, you'll be charged per mile for all excess miles. This can add up quickly, so if you drive more than the average 15,000 miles per year, leasing might not be a smart choice.

Driving Smart

MILEAGE NEGOTIATION In some cases, if you know you'll be exceeding the standard mileage allowance, you can opt before your lease begins to increase the allowance in your lease agreement for a lower per-mile fee than you'd pay later for going above the allowance. Also, miles purchased in advance can be added to the monthly lease fee and amortized over the length of the lease, which makes it easier on the budget than paying a lump sum at lease end.

Yet another potential drawback to leasing is that because you don't own the vehicle, you are not allowed to make any modifications to it. For example, you can't upgrade the stereo system, repaint the vehicle, or add any after-market accessories. The configuration of the vehicle must be kept the same. Otherwise, you'll be charged extra fees to restore the vehicle to its original condition.

The concept of owning a vehicle appeals more to some people, especially those who tend to develop an emotional bond with their car. For these people, leasing may not be a good choice.

Finally, leasing may not even be possible for you. Unless your credit is above average or excellent, you will probably have a difficult time leasing a vehicle. The leasing companies are much stricter when making approval decisions and often approve only people with above-average or excellent credit. If your credit score is below average (less than 675, for example), leasing a vehicle may not be an option. You will probably have a much better chance at getting approved to finance the purchase of a used vehicle, if you're willing to pay an interest rate above average and make a down payment of 10 to 20 percent (or more), depending on your credit score and the lender.

The Difference Between Buying and Leasing

There are similarities between leasing and buying. However, in some important ways, leasing is also very different from buying. When you lease, the dealership is not the leasing company; it's just acting as an agent for the leasing company. You won't start dealing with the leasing company until you make your first monthly payment.

New car dealerships are franchises that are authorized by one or more manufacturers to offer those vehicles. For example, a Honda dealership is authorized to sell (you guessed it) Honda vehicles. In many cases, the vehicle manufacturer has established a subsidiary that serves as the leasing agent. For example, GM has its General Motors Acceptance Corporation (GMAC).

As an alternative to leasing through a new car dealership acting as agent for a leasing company, you can opt to work with a dealership to choose your vehicle and then find a leasing company (such as a bank, a credit union, or an independent leasing company). In some cases, you may be able to get a better deal and save money by doing this. However, new car dealerships, because of existing relationships with leasing companies, make it much easier to lease a vehicle by handling all of the arrangements through the companies they represent.

One of the differences between leasing a vehicle and buying it is that when you lease, you can to select the new car and negotiate your best price for that vehicle, but once approved by a leasing company, it's the leasing company that then purchases the vehicle from the dealership on your behalf. You're then responsible for paying the monthly lease fee to the leasing agent.

Another difference between leasing and purchasing is responsibilities. When you lease a vehicle, you're responsible for making monthly payments for the term of the lease. You're also responsible for insuring that vehicle and paying taxes and licensing fees. In addition, you're responsible for doing what's necessary to maintain the vehicle. At the end of your lease, you return the vehicle in good condition (or pay for any damage beyond the acceptable normal wear) and simply walk away.

Driving Smart

PURCHASE AGREEMENT In some cases, you can opt to purchase the lease vehicle at lease end, for a special price negotiated in advance. However, this arrangement is rarely financially worthwhile for the lessee.

On the other hand, when you own a car, you can decide to sell it at any time. In contrast, when you lease you sign a commitment to make monthly payments for the term of the lease. If you terminate the lease for any reason, you must pay an early termination fee and you're still responsible for making all remaining monthly payments, whether you continue to drive the vehicle or not.

One final difference between leasing and buying is finality. When you sign a lease agreement, the deal is legally binding. You do not have a three-day rescission period or the opportunity to change your mind after driving the vehicle for a while. Once you sign the paperwork, you're legally and financially committed to the lease for the entire term.

Getting out of a Lease Early

In some circumstances, if you are unable to meet the financial obligations of the lease, there are independent lease transfer companies that can help you find someone to take over the lease for you. However, when a lease is transferred, the initial lessee seldom if ever winds up ahead financially.

Some popular lease transfer companies are Swapalease (*www.swapalease.com*) and TakeMyPayments.com (*www.takemy payments.com*). These companies will handle all of the paperwork and details on your behalf, for a fee. Before working with a lease transfer company, check to make sure it's reputable.

Driving Smart

TAKING OVER A LEASE If you want to lease a vehicle for less than two or three years, you might consider taking over someone else's lease. This type of deal often comes with attractive incentives, since lessees who are working with a lease transfer company are typically eager to get out of their leases. The process of transferring a lease to another party is called *subleasing*.

Not all leasing companies allow for their leases to be transferred. Those that do tend to charge a hefty processing fee for the privilege, plus they must approve the new lessee before the transfer can be finalized. The decision to get out of a lease should be a last option.

Meet Leasing Expert Al Hearn

Al Hearn is the editor-in-chief and owner of LeaseGuide.com, a very popular Web site for independent and unbiased vehicle leasing information. In addition to offering comprehensive leasing information in the form of an interactive, 15-chapter e-book, which is available free of charge, LeaseGuide.com offers an inexpensive Leasing Kit ($19.95), which contains all of the tools and information you need to move through the entire leasing process and get the best possible deal.

LeaseGuide.com offers an abundance of information for anyone interested in leasing a vehicle. In this interview, Hearn shares some of his knowledge and experience.

What exactly does LeaseGuide.com offer?

Al Hearn: "I come from a corporate background. During my years working in the corporate world, I developed extensive knowledge about leasing. Because I understood leasing, I understood the benefits and pitfalls. I soon realized, however, that my friends and family didn't share my understanding of leasing. I saw them making serious mistakes when leasing vehicles on their own as consumers.

"Back in 1995, I initially created a Web site to share my knowledge of leasing. When I retired from the corporate world, I began dedicating myself full-time to the ongoing development and expansion of LeaseGuide.com. Over time, the site has grown and improved exponentially.

"On the Web site, the 15-part interactive e-book, which I call *The Lease Guide*, covers everything a consumer needs to know in order to make intelligent decisions about leasing a vehicle. The e-book and the site focus on who should lease and who shouldn't, plus they explain how to calculate a lease payment. I want readers to be able to understand and plan their leases ahead of time, plus avoid common mistakes associated with leasing. In addition to the e-book content, there are dozens of informative articles on the site, all of which are free of charge to Web surfers.

"The premium tool offered on LeaseGuide.com is The Lease Kit, which has a one-time fee of $19.95 associated with acquiring and using it. This is a fully interactive product that walks someone through the entire leasing process, step by step, and includes a variety of different online-based calculators and tools designed to help the lessee save money and improve their understanding of how a lease works. One tool offered in The Lease Kit is the Lease Evaluator, which allows you to quickly plug in numbers offered by the dealer to determine if the leasing deal being offered is a good one or not. If the deal is not a good one, the Lease Evaluator explains why in very easy-to-understand terms."

Is all of the information on LeaseGuide.com unbiased?

Al Hearn: "Yes. The site itself receives revenues from displaying Google Ad word ads, as well as by utilizing affiliate links to certain leasing companies and car-related Web sites. However, the site itself is not affiliated or associated with any vehicle manufacturer, leasing company, bank, credit union, or financial institution. It's totally independent and privately owned. The information is intended to be unbiased; however, the content on the site is definitely pro-leasing, since that's what the Web site is all about. While the site is pro-leasing, it does offer extensive information pertaining to the reasons why leasing is not always the best option for people."

In your opinion, who is the perfect candidate to lease a vehicle rather than purchase one?

Al Hearn: "Someone who has cash, but wants to conserve it. A lessee should be someone with a good credit history and good credit score, and someone who has a stable lifestyle. Leases are intended to be completed. It's very costly and troublesome to end a lease early. If someone anticipates a divorce, illness, loss of a job, or a drop in their income during the potential term of the lease, they should not consider leasing. Once you accept a leased vehicle and have signed the leasing agreement, you're committing to keep that exact vehicle and make all of the monthly payments associated with the lease."

What are some of the drawbacks someone should consider before leasing a vehicle?

Al Hearn: "The possibility of having to end the lease early is a huge drawback. Many people take on a lease without understanding how it works. They're then very surprised by the limitations and costs associated with it. For example, upon signing the lease, they didn't realize they're responsible for paying for excessive mileage or excessive wear and tear on the vehicle, and wind up with a huge bill at the end of the lease period which they weren't anticipating. People need to understand all of the fees and charges associated with leasing a vehicle and calculate them into their budget to avoid unpleasant surprises. Many people enter into leasing after focusing only on one factor, which is the size of the monthly payment. This is a common mistake. Don't be attracted by a low monthly payment if you plan to drive more than 15,000 miles per year, you want to alter or customize the vehicle, or you tend to put excessive wear and tear on a vehicle as a result of your driving habits."

Aside from the initial price of the vehicle, can a lessee negotiate any other part of a lease?

Al Hearn: "Usually not. Most people lease a vehicle through a new car dealership, which is acting only as the leasing agent or middleman. While the lessee negotiates the price of their vehicle, they're given a take-it-or-leave-it lease agreement by the leasing company. A dealership might work with several leasing companies and be able to offer you several alternative leasing deals, but you'll need to select one of those deals and accept its terms as they're spelled out in the agreement."

Do you recommend working with the leasing company represented by their new car dealership or seeking out an independent leasing company?

Al Hearn: "In my opinion, working with a leasing company associated with the dealership and/or manufacturer is almost always the easiest thing to do. The manufacturer is interested in moving vehicles. The lease terms offered by the leasing company that is affiliated with the manufacturer will often offer much better deals than competing independent leasing companies."

What would you say is the biggest problem people encounter when they lease a vehicle?

Al Hearn: "They enter into the leasing process without enough understanding of how a vehicle lease works and they wind up agreeing to something that isn't in their best interests financially. Someone might understand perfectly how to negotiate the best deal possible when purchasing a vehicle and acquiring financing, but they may have no knowledge whatsoever about how to negotiate the best lease deal possible. These two things are not at all the same.

Just because the monthly payment of a lease is lower than the monthly payment associated with financing the purchase of a vehicle, this does not automatically mean you're getting a better deal by leasing. You could easily wind up agreeing to a purchase price that is higher than the vehicle's sticker price and an interest rate that is higher than the national average."

What does someone need to understand about the residual value of a vehicle as it pertains to a lease?

Al Hearn: "It would be nice if they knew the residual that the dealer is going to offer them, which is a figure that's passed along from the leasing company. The residual value of a particular make and model vehicle can change almost on a daily basis and isn't typically something that's readily disclosed before someone initiates the leasing process. Through research, however, a lessee can estimate residual values and make more educated decisions. The residual value that's offered combined with the money factor and any factory-to-dealer or consumer rebates offered are some of what will ultimately determine whether or not a leasing deal is a good one. Without a tool like the Evaluator found on the LeaseGuide.com Web site, it's hard to determine if a potential lease deal is a good one."

Based on your knowledge and experience, are there certain vehicle makes that are better to lease than others?

Al Hearn: "Most luxury vehicles, like Mercedes-Benz, BMW, Lexus, and Acura, all have great lease residuals because the luxury vehicles tend to hold their values better than other vehicles. Toyotas and Hondas are also known for holding their value."

When, if ever, does it make sense to purchase a vehicle after the lease is over?

Al Hearn: "Typically, purchasing a car at the end of a lease is not a good deal. The residual value of the vehicle at the end of the lease is typically higher than the actual market value of the now-used vehicle. You're almost always better off returning the leased vehicle and then researching the Kelley Blue Book value of that now-used vehicle, and then purchasing the same exact make, model, and year vehicle elsewhere."

In your opinion, is there a best time of year to lease a vehicle?

Al Hearn: "It used to be that you'd get the best deals at the end of a model year or at the end of a month when a dealership is trying to meet its sales quota. These days, car manufacturers are constantly offering special promotions, rebates, and incentives of all kinds, which are made available at various times of the year. Generally, you can get a better deal at the beginning of a new model year if you're interested in leasing last year's model, for example. Visiting a dealer at the end of a month when they're trying to meet their quota also sometimes still works."

Do you have any other advice for someone interested in leasing a vehicle?

Al Hearn: "Yes, but it's the same advice I would give to someone who is buying a car. The advice is to do plenty of research about the exact car you want and what features you want that vehicle to have. Part of this research should include test-driving different vehicles that could meet your needs and that are within your budget. Once you know what new vehicle you're looking for, do further research to get the best possible pricing for it. Obtain the vehicle's MSRP and invoice price. I recommend also getting the Edmunds True Market Value price, which is available from the Edmunds.com Web site. Do your research and never rely on a salesperson or dealership to provide you with the education you need or the information you'll want to have before entering into a negotiation to purchase or lease a vehicle."

Always Do Your Research!

Throughout this book, the importance of doing research is emphasized heavily, whether you're buying or leasing. One of the best ways to do this research, while staying in the comfort of your home or office, is to use the Internet. The next chapter offers detailed information about useful and popular car-related Web sites that can make your research easy. In Chapter 8, you'll then read interviews with several additional car experts who are affiliated with some of these popular Web sites.

Driving Smart

FEE OR NO FEE In most cases, the information offered on the popular car-related Web sites is free of charge. When low, one-time fees are charged, it's so you can quickly obtain proprietary information or data that could potentially save you hundreds or even thousands of dollars when purchasing or leasing a car.

7

Online Car Shopping

WHAT'S IN THIS CHAPTER

- Why cyberspace is the perfect place to shop for a vehicle
- Doing online research to find the best vehicle for you
- The top car-related Web sites worth visiting

W hen buying a new or used car, selling a used car, or leasing a car, one of the very best tools at your disposal—24/7/365—is the Internet. On the Web there are literally hundreds of informative car-related sites you can use as resources to make various aspects of your vehicle selection and buying process easier. Using the Web, you can do the following:

- Find the best car financing deals for which your credit score and credit history qualify you.
- Purchase genuine and third-party vehicle accessories.
- Research the most affordable insurance rates.
- Research new and used vehicle makes and models, comparing vehicles feature by feature to determine which is best for you.
- Learn all about the specific make and model vehicle you're interested in (including its safety and customer satisfaction rating).
- Search for the best deal possible on a new or used vehicle by getting multiple dealers to offer quotes via e-mail.
- Sell your current vehicle privately in order to get top dollar for it.
- Find a reputable dealer in your area that has the car you want in stock.

With the power of the Internet, important research that used to require hours of hard work now takes just minutes. When you go into a dealership armed with the right information, you're more apt to get the best deal possible and drive away in a vehicle that's best suited to meet your needs. The Internet allows you to acquire the right information, often for free. All you need to do is invest a few minutes to access the appropriate Web sites to find the information you want and need.

Driving Smart

LOTS OF SITES In addition to the Web sites described in this chapter, be sure to check the Web sites of the vehicle manufacturers. See Chapter 1 for a listing of Web sites for each of them, from Acura to Volvo.

INSURANCE COMPANIES HAVE SITES, TOO If you're searching for a great deal on automotive insurance, you can quickly compare rates and coverage offered by well-known insurance providers— including Allstate, Progressive, State Farm, and Geico—by visiting the Yahoo! Auto Web site (*autos.yahoo.com/carcenter/car_insurance.html*). More information about shopping for auto insurance and choosing appropriate coverage can be found in Chapter 10.

Doing Online Research to Find the Best Vehicle

There are many Web sites that enable you to perform detailed searches for vehicles based on a wide range of criteria that you select. These sites can help you more easily narrow down the make and model of vehicle that's best suited for you. For example, you can sort based on price, vehicle type, size, passenger capacity, fuel efficiency, safety rating, consumer satisfaction rating, reviews, features, etc. With hundreds of new makes and models and thousands makes and models of used vehicles, using online tools to narrow down your options can save so much time.

Based on what you determined you want and need (from your answers to the questions in Chapter 1), you can narrow down your search online to just a few vehicles and then visit dealerships to test-drive those vehicles. You can also shop online for the lowest price by researching pricing and obtaining quotes from dealers.

Driving Smart

GEOGRAPHY COUNTS Even once you decide on a specific vehicle and select the dealer where you want to buy or lease that vehicle, use the Internet to research the Kelley Blue Book Value, which is the price that people in your geographic area have recently paid for the same vehicle make, model, and year. This will give you an edge in the price negotiation process.

To save time before visiting dealerships, you can visit a Web site such as Cars.com (*www.cars.com*), enter the make and model of a car and your ZIP code, and then build your vehicle online by selecting the configuration, options, and accessories you want. When you've got what you want, you can click on the "Get Quote" icon to find the starting price that local dealers in your area are asking. With that figure, you can open a negotiation with each dealership via e-mail, by telephone, or in person.

The ability to customize a vehicle (select options, color, accessories, etc.) is a feature you'll find at most vehicle manufacturer Web sites (as listed in Chapter 1). When you visit a manufacturer's site, with the click of the mouse you can be referred to one or more local dealerships and have them compete for your business.

What's great about many of the vehicle sites is that they're extremely user-friendly, not only for computer novices, but also for people who know little or nothing about cars. Thus, many of these Web sites (including those operated by the manufacturers) can be wonderful learning tools.

The Top Car-Related Web Sites Worth Checking

There are hundreds of informative, car-related Web sites. The challenge in doing research is to locate a few sites that offer timely, accurate, and useful information in a format you can understand easily.

No matter what type of vehicle information you need, chances are you'll find it on one of the Web sites described in this chapter. Each site listed in this chapter offers a wide range of tools to help you conduct research, find the best possible

---

Driving Smart

WORTH THE MONEY While much of the information you'll want and need is available free of charge, some of these sites offer fee-based services that can help you save a fortune over time. For example, if you're shopping for a used car, purchasing a Carfax report for a specific vehicle can help you learn all about its history and discover if the seller is being honest about any accidents, for example. Paying a small fee for certain information can save you hundreds, perhaps thousands of dollars.

---

deals (on vehicles, accessories, financing, and/or insurance), and gather the knowledge you need before visiting dealerships, taking test-drives, and ultimately selecting the vehicle to purchase or lease.

Driving Smart

CAR MAGAZINE SITES In addition to these Web sites, take advantage of the many car magazines and printed car pricing guides you'll find at virtually all bookstores and newsstands. These publications cover the very latest new vehicles and provide pricing information, whether you're buying a new or used vehicle or selling your current vehicle.

The following sites are among the most useful, reliable, accurate, and informative on the Web, of interest to anyone planning to buy or lease a vehicle. You'll probably only need to visit a few of these sites (listed alphabetically) to acquire the knowledge you seek.

American Automobile Association (AAA)

www.aaa.com

This site offers vehicle buying tools, car reviews and ratings, insurance information, vehicle financing referrals and discounts, referrals for local mechanics, and other money-saving services. AAA membership is not required to access many of the resources on this site.

Autobytel

www.autobytel.com

This is a comprehensive, free resource for anyone buying a

vehicle, new or used. If you're shopping for a new vehicle, Autobytel can help you to quickly compare vehicles, access detailed car reviews, and obtain price quotes from dealerships in your area—all without leaving your home or office. If you're shopping for a used vehicle, you can quickly search through a nationwide database containing listings for thousands of vehicles, including certified pre-owned (CPO) vehicles. Visitors to this site can also access Kelley Blue Book pricing data, watch informative videos about the newest cars, and access customer alert and recall information from all vehicle manufacturers.

AutoCheck

www.autocheck.com

This service enables you to do a comprehensive background check on any used vehicle using its vehicle identification number (VIN). There is a fee for using this service, but it can save you a fortune and protect you from being misled by a dealer or a private seller. A background check can tell you if a vehicle has been involved in any major accidents and if the odometer has been tampered with (a crime, of course). You can also learn about whoever has owned a title on the vehicle and if a vehicle has been part of a rental car fleet or if it had only one owner. Before buying a used car, it's definitely smart to run a check on the VIN, either with Autocheck or with Carfax.com or similar services. Autocheck is a service offered by Experian, one of the three credit reporting agencies.

CAR SPEAK **VEHICLE IDENTIFICATION NUMBER (VIN)**—This is a unique serial number given to every vehicle manufactured and imprinted on the vehicle. The VIN is used to register the vehicle with the state Department of Motor Vehicles or Registry of Motor Vehicles. It can be used to track a vehicle's history.

BANKRATE.COM

www.bankrate.com

This is a personal finance site that offers a vast amount of financial information of interest to consumers. Here, you can learn about the latest vehicle financing rates. Bankrate.com is useful if you're shopping for the most competitive vehicle financing deal. You can learn which banks, credit unions, and lenders are offering the best deals, quickly compare rates and fees, and learn how to save money on financing when buying a vehicle. On the home page, click on the "Auto" icon. Informative articles and online tools to help you plan your financing are among the resources offered on this site, which is supported by advertising and free of charge to access. One online tool will help you determine if you can afford your dream car, using various financing options. Another tool will help you calculate your monthly car payment, while a third will help you determine whether buying or leasing makes more financial sense in your particular situation.

Car and Driver

www.caranddriver.com

An online edition of *Car and Driver* magazine, this site offers news, reviews, and information about new cars plus a detailed car buying guide. If you want to learn about all of the latest cars and then compare vehicles feature by feature, read detailed reviews, and learn which vehicles the editors of *Car and Driver* believe are the best and worst of the current model year, check out this Web site.

Cars.com

www.cars.com

This is a guide to new and used cars, which contains detailed information about all makes and models of vehicles and listings for thousands of used cars currently for sale across the United States. This site offers an abundance of tools and information of interest to anyone considering buying a car. Dealer referrals, online price quotes, Kelley Blue Book pricing, and a loan calculator are among the features here. The site's Top 10 lists will help you learn which vehicles have the best and worst gas mileage and resale value, which are the most popular among consumers, and which have the best crash test ratings. This is an advertiser-supported site that's free of charge to use.

CARFAX

www.carfax.com

Similar in functionality to AutoCheck, the CARFAX site enables you to quickly obtain detailed information about the history of any used car, based on its VIN. You can determine if the car has been in any accidents, who has owned it, whether it has ever been totaled or classified as a lemon or salvage, or if the odometer has been tampered with. Before purchasing any used car, whether through a dealer or a private seller, it's smart to obtain a CARFAX report for it. CARFAX is definitely the most trusted source for vehicle histories. All you need to get started is the VIN.

Driving Smart

DON'T RELY ON DEALERS Never rely on a CARFAX or AutoCheck report provided by a dealer or private seller. Obtain the vehicle's VIN and purchase a report on that car for yourself. Some less reputable dealers (and private sellers) have been known to falsify reports to make vehicles more marketable. You can purchase single reports or, for a flat fee, an unlimited number of CARFAX or AutoCheck reports for under $25, so it's easy to learn about all of the used vehicles you're considering. The reports are easy to read, but extremely comprehensive.

Consumer Reports

www.consumerreports.org/cro/cars/index.htm

The editors of *Consumer Reports* offer detailed reviews and information of interest to anyone buying a new or used vehicle. In addition to reviews and information about all new cars on the market, this site enables users to research used vehicles and access information about the safety record and crash test ratings for virtually all makes and models. You can learn which vehicles are best in their class based on price, fuel efficiency, safety, owner satisfaction, luxury, and various other criteria. You can also learn about the ten worst cars in terms of depreciation and learn about new features and options available in the latest cars. Like the *Consumer Reports* magazine, the information on this Web site is totally unbiased. It's also timely, accurate, and free of charge to access. The site also offers dealership referrals, online price quotes, and the ability to research financing options. Additional features are available to paid subscribers of the magazine.

Edmunds

www.edmunds.com

A comprehensive resource for learning about new and used vehicles, this site offers detailed vehicle descriptions and online buyer's guides. An exclusive feature is True Market Value®, a proprietary system for calculating what others are paying for new and used vehicles, based on real sales data from your geographic area. This is extremely valuable for getting pricing information before entering into negotiations with any dealer for any vehicle, new or used. Like other car-related Web sites, this one also offers top-ten lists and informative articles that can help you shop more wisely.

Kelley Blue Book

www.kbb.com

This site features timely, accurate, and comprehensive new and used car pricing information from one of the most trusted sources in the automotive industry.

In addition to offering news, reviews, and information about thousands of new and used makes and models, this site offers vehicle pricing information that dealers and consumers have relied upon since 1918. Using this site, you can research pricing for a specific make and model or compare vehicles in a specific price range or by category. You can also obtain price quotes from local dealers, learn about rebates and other incentives currently offered by various manufacturers, access safety ratings for any make and model, and learn about your financing and insurance options. Up-to-date and reliable pricing information for any vehicles of interest will give you a tremendous advantage when negotiating with dealers or private sellers. When you request new vehicle pricing information from the Kelley Blue Book Web site, you give the make, manufacturer, and year of a vehicle and you'll get the vehicle's MSRP, invoice price, and New Car Blue Book Value (what consumers are paying for this vehicle). You'll also be able to view a summary of the vehicle's features, read the official Blue Book review of the vehicle (which includes the JD Power Quality Rating), see a list of dealers in your area selling the vehicle, and be able to obtain a price quote. In addition to this site, the Kelley Blue Book printed directories are extremely useful for anyone shopping for a vehicle.

National Automobile Dealers Association (NADA)

www.nada.org / *www.nadaguides.com*

While NADA is a professional trade organization representing dealers, this site offers consumers tools and information that can help them shop for vehicles. To get started from *www.nada.org*, click on the "Find a Car" option. From *www.nadaguides.com*, you can access a vast amount of information about all makes and models of new and used vehicles, search listings for used vehicles currently for sale, compare vehicles based on features or other criteria, and learn about new vehicles from all popular manufacturers. Of course, you can also obtain referrals for local new and used dealerships and learn about the code of ethics this organization enforces among its members.

Vehix.com

www.vehix.com

On this site you can learn about new and used vehicles through interactive, multimedia buyer's guides to new and used cars. This site enables you to access a vast database of used cars available for sale (searchable by many criteria, including ZIP code).

Yahoo! Autos

autos.yahoo.com

It makes sense that one of the world's most popular Internet search engines would offer one of the Web's most comprehensive online resources for information on new and used vehicles. From this site, you can learn about and shop for the best auto financing deals and insurance. This site offers new and used car reviews, unique 360-degree visual tours of the interior and exterior of many vehicles, information about current rebates and other incentives, Kelley Blue Book pricing data, and the ability to obtain online price quotes from participating new and used dealers nationwide. This site also offers detailed information about "green vehicles," including a comprehensive buyer's guide to hybrid cars.

Driving Smart

SHOPPING FOR PARTS If you're shopping for genuine or third-party parts or accessories, you can find the lowest prices and best deals using a price comparison Web site. Simply visit one of these sites, enter the exact part or accessory you want, and then find companies that are selling it for the lowest price. Popular price comparison sites include Shopzilla (*www.shopzilla.com*), NexTag (*www.nextag.com*), and PriceGrabber.com (*www.pricegrabber.com*).

MORE ON HYBRIDS To learn all about hybrid vehicles and how you can help protect the environment, check out HybridCars.com (*www.hybrid cars.com*). Also, read the exclusive interview with Bradley Berman, the site's founder, in Chapter 11.

Learn from Experienced Car Experts

In addition to the information you'll find on the Web sites listed in this chapter, you'll learn from the car experts who provide content to these sites by reading the exclusive, in-depth interviews featured in the next chapter. These interviews offer additional tips and strategies for buying or leasing a new or used vehicle and a variety of perspectives on buying and leasing.

Auto Experts Share Their Secrets

WHAT'S IN THIS CHAPTER

- Exclusive interviews with auto industry experts
- Learn how to shop for and negotiate the best price for any vehicle

N ow that you've learned about some of the most popular car-related Web sites (Chapter 7), here's an opportunity to learn more about buying vehicles. From
these exclusive interviews with the experts in charge of providing content for some of these sites, you'll learn additional
tips for shopping and for getting the lowest possible price.

Jack Nerad

Executive Editorial Director
Kelley Blue Book
www.kbb.com

For determining vehicle values and resale prices and what
other buyers are paying for new and used vehicles, there's no
better known or more authoritative source than Kelley Blue
Book. The company offers its information in printed directories, through its Web site, and through partnerships with
other vehicle information resources.

Jack Nerad is the executive editor at Kelley Blue Book, as
well as the co-host of *America on the Road*, a national radio
show that airs on over 300 stations across the United States.
He's also served as the editor of *Motor Trend* magazine. In this
interview, Nerad shares his advice for better understanding
vehicle pricing and getting the best deal possible when buying a new or used vehicle.

**What is Kelley Blue Book and what services does the com-
pany offers to consumers?**

Jack Nerad: "Kelley Blue Book has an 80-year history of providing price and value information to dealers, consumers, OEMs [original equipment manufacturers], and financial institutions. For the first 70 years of the company's existence, it published trade pricing guides for the automotive industry. About 10 years ago, we put this information online and made it available to consumers, which literally transformed the way cars are now bought and sold in America."

What does someone shopping for a new or used vehicle really need to know about pricing?

Jack Nerad: "They need to know what people are actually paying in the marketplace. There's a lot of confusion among consumers when it comes to vehicle pricing, particularly in terms of new vehicles. Consumers are confronted with the MSRP, which is displayed on the Monroney label, or sticker price. Most people know they should not have to pay the sticker price for a vehicle, but they're not sure what do to. Some consumers can take advantage of the dealer invoice price, which is essentially what the dealership is paying for the vehicle, so that can help with price negotiations. The problem is, the dealer invoice price does not reflect various manufacturer incentives, which could add up to several thousand dollars of additional profit for a dealership. People also don't know what type of mark-up a dealer should get or is entitled to.

"One piece of information we at Kelley Blue Book offer to consumers is what we call the New Car Blue Book Value Price. This is the price that people are typically paying in the marketplace. This price is based on the vehicle as you choose to equip it and it's localized to your geographic area. So, using this information, you'll get a good idea of what other customers in your area have recently paid, after their own negotiations, for the exact vehicle you want to purchase. Armed with this information, a consumer will have much greater negotiation power."

What mistakes do consumers commonly make in pricing a vehicle?

Jack Nerad: "Instead of focusing on the actual price of the vehicle, they consider only the monthly payment that will be associated with that vehicle. They don't pay attention to how much they're actually going to pay for the vehicle over the life of the loan, including interest charges. I recommend using an online payment calculator found on Web sites like *kbb.com*. Of course, by extending the term of the loan, you can make a monthly car payment lower, but you're also increasing the total price of the vehicle, because you're paying more interest over time."

How do dealer incentives and rebates impact the price of a vehicle?

Jack Nerad: "Rebates and incentives can impact the price of a vehicle heavily. Often, you can buy a vehicle at invoice price;

however, the dealer can still be making a lot of money, because the manufacturer could be offering factory-to-dealer cash incentives that as a consumer you don't necessarily know about. If you did know about these incentives, you could negotiate more tactically and save 10 to 20 percent of the purchase price. If you're a savvy negotiator, you can sometimes pay a price that's lower than the dealer invoice price. One way to find out about current incentives and rebates is to use our Web site. We maintain a comprehensive listing of incentives being offered regionally for all new vehicle makes and models. You can obtain this information online in minutes."

What negotiation strategy should a buyer use with a dealership?

Jack Nerad: "I'd have to say that any consumer's best negotiation edge is their ability to walk out the door at any time during the negotiation. No matter what type of new or used vehicle you're shopping for, chances are there are other nearby dealerships or private sellers offering a comparable vehicle at a more competitive price. The marketplace is hotly competitive for both new and used cars. If you're not liking what you're hearing from a dealer or you're not getting the price you're willing to pay based on your research, walk away and seek out that same vehicle elsewhere if the seller is refusing to lower their price.

"I recommend shopping around for competitive prices. You can either visit each dealer separately or request price quotes online or via the telephone. From our Web site, you can obtain price quotes from multiple nearby dealerships by making one single online request. When requesting a quote, make sure you specifically ask for the make, model, year, and vehicle configuration you're looking for. Be very specific. There are a lot of ways to get dealers competing with each other for your business. That's how you're going to get the best price.

"Be aware that some dealers will offer an online or telephone price quote, but when you show up to their dealership, they'll want to add to that price. If this happens, be prepared to walk away if the original quoted price isn't honored. After you receive a price quote from a dealer, you can always negotiate further."

At what point should a buyer stop negotiating with a dealer and accept the price being offered?

Jack Nerad: "That's a good question with no easy answer. The key is to do your research, so you know the value of the vehicle and what others have recently paid for it. Also, be aware of what incentives or rebates the dealer is being offered by the manufacturer on that sale. You can negotiate on and on, but at some point, you need to consider how much haggling over that last $50 or $100 is really worth to you, especially if you're financing the vehicle for three to five years. If you can get a price in the ballpark of what you know the average consumer has recently paid for the same vehicle, that's a reasonable time to stop negotiating.

"Typically, when you negotiate a vehicle price, you're negotiating for the vehicle configured exactly the way you want it, including all of your selected options and accessories. I do not recommend negotiating the price of every option or accessory separately. That's just not time-productive. Select your vehicle and how you want it configured, and then start negotiating the price."

Is there a difference between negotiating the price for a new car and negotiating the price for a used car?

Jack Nerad: "Yes. Typically, there's more of a margin in a used car. This, however, may be different if you're dealing with a private seller versus a dealership. In the used car game, there are now fixed-priced superstores, which refuse to negotiate on their prices. The price displayed on the vehicle is what they'll sell it for. If you don't care for the negotiation thing, this is one option for buying a used vehicle. I always recommend doing a lot of homework before purchasing a used vehicle. This research takes just minutes and is almost always free. Much of the information you need to know about a used car can be found on a Web site like *www.kbb.com*."

What are some of the other ways a Website *like kbb.com* can help a person buy a new or used vehicle?

Jack Nerad: "Our Web site, as well as others, allows you to quickly compare various makes and models of cars, plus compare features and prices with ease. This allows you to quickly narrow down your search. We also offer detailed reviews for specific new and used vehicle makes/models, plus tips for helping you negotiate the best price for your vehicle.

"When buying a new or used car, there are four separate transactions involved. I recommend keeping these transactions separate, even if the dealership tries to combine some or all of them. These transactions are choosing and buying the specific vehicle, trading in or selling your existing vehicle, obtaining financing, and buying insurance. From a financial standpoint, each of these transactions should be considered separate."

What are some of the biggest mistakes people make when shopping for a vehicle?

Jack Nerad: "They make the mistake of falling in love with a specific vehicle and transform the process into a totally emotional decision. It's important to remember that in addition to being able to seek out other dealerships or sellers to acquire a specific make/model of car, for every vehicle there are also one or more comparable options available from other manufacturers. Knowing this, try to take the emotions out of the buying process and focus on making rational decisions, based on price, features, safety, and quality, for example.

"A lot of people aren't too rational when comparing lease options versus purchase options for the same vehicle.

Many people will look at the lease option and see it comes with a lower monthly payment, then assume it's a better deal. This is rarely the case. Whether or not leasing a vehicle makes sense depends a lot on your personal circumstances.

"I have seen research showing that someone purchasing a vehicle will only visit 1.2 to 1.5 dealerships when shopping for the best deal. This indicates that a whole lot of people are just walking into a dealership and making a deal on the spot. That's not the best way to price shop."

Should a person shopping for a used vehicle consider a certified pre-owned vehicle?

Jack Nerad: "Certified pre-owned vehicles generally are priced at a premium, because they come with various extras, such as a more comprehensive warranty or a better financing offer. Before purchasing a CPO, make sure you understand what the premium is you'll be paying and determine if it's worth the extra money. It's really a peace of mind issue, as much as anything else. Most of the benefits associated with a CPO relate to the warranty, which to some consumers is very important."

Overall, what would you say is the biggest misconception people have about shopping for a new or used vehicle and pricing that vehicle?

Jack Nerad: "The biggest misconception is that people think the dealer has all of the power. If you're financially stable and have decent credit, you, as the consumer, have all of the power in the world, especially if you pre-arm yourself with research data and relevant information. There are so many free online tools available to car shoppers. Not only can you learn about vehicle pricing information, you can also access detailed car reviews, safety reports, and other information of interest to buyers. Take advantage of these resources to become an educated consumer. Also, take advantage of the fact that there's heavy competition in the marketplace. There are good deals everywhere, if you're willing to spend the time looking for them."

What's a common mistake that consumers make when shopping for a vehicle?

Jack Nerad: "They allow themselves to be rushed into making a rash decision. Never allow a dealership to rush you for any reason. If you ever feel uncomfortable, walk out the door. You have all of the power. There is always going to be a great choice of vehicles out there waiting for you. If you feel the need to walk out, do it. You'll often be doing yourself a great service, plus you can potentially save money. Also, if you want honesty from the salesperson, be honest yourself. Be honest when expressing your wants, needs, and budget.

"When shopping for a specific vehicle, be consistent and coherent about what you want to buy. Don't go into one dealership requesting one thing, then visit a second dealership and request a quote for a totally different vehicle configuration and then hope to compare the two quotes accurately. Once you pinpoint what you want and need, in terms of the vehicle's make, model, year, and configuration, stick to it and start shopping around for the best price. Compare apples to apples. I would do a lot of my price shopping before I visit actual dealerships."

Are there any ratings available for determining the quality or honesty of a dealership?

Jack Nerad: "Not yet. You can research a specific dealership by contacting the local Better Business Bureau, for example. You can also pay attention to various consumer satisfaction awards the dealership has won. Many of these awards actually mean something. In the future, Kelley Blue Book is looking to offer one coherent rating system for dealerships, but it's not something I can offer too much information on right now.

"If you want accurate information on a specific vehicle, I recommend obtaining a CARFAX vehicle history report for that vehicle—CARFAX is a partner of ours at Kelley Blue Book—or you can visit the CARFAX.com Web site. Our goal at the Kelley Blue Book Web site is to be a one-stop shop for someone looking to research pricing and other information about a vehicle. Our detailed vehicle reviews, for example, can also help you narrow down your options, once you choose a vehicle type."

Brian Chee
Managing Editor
Autobytel
www.autobytel.com

Some popular car-related Web sites focus on helping consumers obtain the most accurate pricing information or vehicle histories, while others offer a broader range of information, including detailed car reviews, to help people select the ideal vehicle and find a dealership to work with. Autobytel.com is one of the popular car-related Web sites designed for people who are shopping for a new or used vehicle and who know little or nothing about cars. For more knowledgeable car enthusiasts, Autobytel.com also offers an abundance of timely, accurate, and informative technical information.

As the managing editor of Autobytel, Brian Chee has become an expert in providing the information that consumers want and need. Chee has been involved in covering the automotive industry as a journalist for over a decade. A car enthusiast, he started writing about and reviewing cars after graduating from journalism school. His career is now centered on the automotive industry.

What does Autobytel.com offer to consumers?

Brian Chee: "Autobytel.com is basically a research and buying resource that offers news, reviews, and feature articles pertaining to new and used vehicles. People can start by reading reviews of vehicles, then obtain referrals for

---

dealerships and get in contact with them online. We merge the power of the Internet to allow people to perform comprehensive research, plus offer an online link to dealerships to help facilitate the negotiating and buying process. Our goal is to make the buying process easier and assist consumers in getting a fair price.

"From a research perspective, Autobytel.com is very tuned into providing a commonsense approach to vehicle information. We take great pains to provide information for the everyday consumer. We offer real-world recommendations for people. When you read a car review, you'll learn how that vehicle will treat you on your daily commute, for example, and how reliable it is. You'll discover how that vehicle will behave when you drive it and how reliable it will be several years in the future. We help consumers discover what they can expect from the vehicle they're interested in. Our coverage utilizes text, photographs, video, and sound to help people obtain the information they need to make a sound buying decision, without getting confused or intimidated. We try to take the important details of a car's performance and present it in a way that anyone can understand."

Who is a typical user of Autobytel.com?

Brian Chee: "It's someone who is actively looking to purchase or lease a new or used vehicle. They know what type of car they want or need, and now they're looking to narrow down their options and choose the best vehicle make and model. People come to Autobytel.com to do research and determine what vehicles will best fit their lives and lifestyle. In addition to offering new car reviews for all makes and models, we have used car reviews going back to 1994."

What tips can you share with someone looking to get the best possible price when shopping for a new vehicle, in addition to knowing about price and vehicle value?

Brian Chee: "By doing research, you can determine how popular a particular make and model is, then determine how long one of those vehicles sits on a dealer's lot before being sold. If you discover a vehicle is extremely popular and in demand, you'll have less negotiating power in terms of price, because the dealer knows that if you walk out the door, someone will be entering right behind you to buy that vehicle. If, however, a vehicle isn't in such hot demand, for whatever reason, or it's been sitting on that dealer's lot for a while, you have a considerable amount of negotiating power. Your negotiating power is based on supply and demand.

"A savvy shopper will also go online and determine which manufacturers are offering incentives, rebates, and special financing deals. These are all opportunities to save a considerable amount of money."

What are some of the biggest misconceptions people have when shopping for a new or used vehicle?

Brian Chee: "I think that perhaps one of the biggest misconceptions is that all vehicles are the same and that there is not a lot of difference between how cars are made and their quality. That's not true and research will show that. Every vehicle meets a different set of quality standards and offers a different driving experience. I am a firm believer in always buying the very best quality vehicle you can afford. With quality comes reliability, which will save you money in the long run. Never buy a bad car because it's cheap. Buy the best car you can afford based on reviews, reliability, and safety ratings and make your decision based on solid data. If you buy a cheap car, but it winds up having to be in the shop often, you won't ultimately save any money, plus it will depreciate in value a lot faster. I recommend researching a vehicle's resale value. Some vehicles hold their values extremely well over time, while others simply do not."

When should someone consider buying a used car rather than a new vehicle?

Brian Chee: "Don't separate the two. If you have $20,000 to spend on a car, look at both new and used vehicles and keep your options open. If you're shopping based on price, you will be able to stretch your dollar further if you purchase a quality used vehicle."

One of the features on the Autobytel.com Web site is a series of top ten lists. How can someone best use the information on these lists?

Brian Chee: "We have a lot of different top ten lists. We take valuable advice and put it into a format that's quick to read, but that also offers the information a consumer needs. The top ten lists take a specific piece of criteria and offer what our research shows to be a consumer's ten best options or choices."

What would you say are some of the worst mistakes people make when buying a new or used vehicle?

Brian Chee: "Buying on impulse is definitely a huge mistake. You might like the way a car looks or the way it drives, but in reality, it might not fit your budget or be something you can ultimately afford. Make sure the vehicle you choose will fit your needs and lifestyle. After you purchase the vehicle, you don't want to ask yourself, 'What was I thinking?' Look at the purchase of a car just like you would any other major purchase. It's an emotional decision, but it's also important to add common sense to your decision-making process. Don't walk into a dealership without doing your research first. Know what the car costs, what rebates are available, what the gas mileage is like, and other information about the vehicle that's of interest to you.

"For efficiency's sake, the most important thing is to truly understand what you expect the car to do and what you'll be using it for. Your needs will be very different if you're looking to transport your family in a minivan, versus needing a car to commute to work. If you know your needs, you can be much more efficient doing your research. If you know what you need and what you want, and understand how these two things can merge, you can quickly narrow down your options.

"Once your options have been narrowed down, focus on what features are important, whether it's fuel efficiency, safety ratings, price, comfort, customer satisfaction ratings, or resale value, for example. You'll find your options will dwindle down to a very manageable selection."

How can someone get the most out of reading vehicle reviews?

Brian Chee: "There is a lot of information out there about all vehicles. I recommend putting that information into context. One way to do this is to read professional reviews. A professional review is written by an expert who knows what to look for when evaluating an automobile. If you read several different reviews and get a handful of different and totally independent opinions about a vehicle, you'll be able to make more intelligent decisions about which vehicles truly offer the best value, best overall performance, and most enjoyable driving experience.

"Most people can read a vast amount of technical information about a vehicle, but they don't understand how that data translates into real life. By reading professional reviews, experts can help you take that technical information and put it into proper context in a way that relates to you and your needs. Being able to apply technical information to real-world scenarios is very valuable information."

Through your work with Autobytel.com, you have become an expert on hybrid vehicles. What should someone know about these vehicles before shopping for one?

Brian Chee: "Buying a hybrid vehicle is all about making a statement. It's not necessarily about saving money. In fact, you'll probably pay more initially for a hybrid vehicle and it could take up to five years or longer to break even on that investment, if you compare it with the cost of a traditional vehicle. It's a good thing that people are buying hybrids. It makes a statement that the automotive industry and federal government are paying attention to.

"Hybrids are extremely efficient and are excellent vehicles. Most of them deliver on the promise that you see when you read the ads. They're clean burning and well-built and they offer a nice driving experience. What I would say, however, is that unless you're willing to pay more for that car, do not rush into the purchase of a hybrid vehicle based on a purely emotional decision. Right now, hybrid vehicles are trendy. But, like any popular vehicle, you'll have a tough time finding them at a discount.

"Right now, even if you add up all of the people who drive hybrid vehicles, the impact on overall gas consumption and on the protection of the environment is minimal, at best. As of 2006, hybrid vehicles currently only made up about 1.5 percent of the overall vehicle market. Many more people drive older vehicles that are not at all fuel-efficient. Again, I believe driving a hybrid is all about making a statement. It's making the public and the industry pay more attention to the fuel efficiency of all vehicles.

"There are definitely some hybrid vehicles out there that are better than others in terms of fuel efficiency versus performance. The term 'hybrid' applies to cars that are efficient and that don't emit a lot of pollutants. A hybrid is nothing more than a vehicle with a different type of power train. It's a gas-powered car that's combined with an electric motor and a battery to store energy. Hybrid is the connection of two different power sources into one power train. It does not always refer directly to fuel efficiency."

Mark Perleberg

Lead Automotive Expert, NADAguides.com
Co-Host, *Car and Driver Radio* and *Road and Track Radio*
www.nadaguides.com
At age 12, Mark Perleberg began working at his older brother's car dealership as a lot attendant. He later trained to become a mechanic and eventually worked as the sales manager of his brother's dealership. In 1980, he became the sales manager and used car manager for a dealership that owned five franchises in four locations. In 1983, he started a business wholesaling cars. Until 2001, he was selling approximately 2,000 cars per year through his company.

Perleberg has also served as the "collector car" editor for Kelley Blue Book and now holds the title of "lead automotive expert" for NADA Guides. He's also the co-host of the *Car and Driver* and *Road and Track* radio shows, which are both nationally syndicated in over 100 U.S. markets.

What are the NADA Guides and how are they affiliated with NADA, the National Automotive Dealers Association?

Mark Perleberg: "NADA is the professional association that fights for the rights of the franchised car dealers. It serves as a buffer between the car dealerships and the factories. NADA Guides publishes guidebooks, plus operates two Web sites. One is a business-to-business site and the other is a business-to-consumer site, which is the one I work on. The Nadaguides.com Web site is an independent vehicle pricing and information source for consumers. I personally write a lot of automobile reviews and how-to articles for the Web site. Our goal is to help consumers weave their way through the car-buying process."

Based on your experience as a car dealer and automotive journalist, what can average consumers do to get the best deal possible when shopping for a car?

Mark Perleberg: "The first thing they can do is figure out what they really want, based on their driving habits and lifestyle. If the consumers do their research and are educated about the car-buying or -leasing process, it makes it a lot easier for them as well as the dealer to match them up with the ideal vehicle.

"I also recommend not bothering to negotiate with a dealer on the price of a car until you're one hundred percent sure you've found the car you're interested in buying or leasing. Don't haggle for something you don't want. It just wastes everyone's time. Figure out what type of car fits your needs and what your needs may be over the next few years. If you're planning to have a second or third child in two years, will the car you're buying or leasing today have enough capacity for your family as it grows?

"Before buying or leasing a car, ask yourself if it's really the car you see yourself in. Also, don't settle for a blue car if you had your heart set on a green one. Find a vehicle that will make you happy. If you get the vehicle you really want, you'll be satisfied a lot longer. That last thing you want is to be driving down the road in a year or two from now, see another car and say to yourself, 'That's the vehicle I really wanted.' Getting an awesome deal on a vehicle you don't really want isn't really a good deal after all.

"Another important thing a consumer can do is be mindful of their credit score and credit history. The information will impact their ability to get competitive financing or a lease. If your credit score is low, spend a few months taking steps to improve it before you start car shopping. An average or above-average credit score can potentially save you thousands in finance charges and interest on an auto loan over a three- or five-year period.

"If your credit score is low, the dealer will be forced to offer you a high interest rate on your loan. This is not their fault; it's yours. If you're offered a high interest rate, don't automatically assume you're being ripped off by the dealership or the financing company. Do your own research so you know what rates you actually qualify for."

What specific tools are available to car shoppers on the NADAguides.com Web site that can't be found elsewhere?

Mark Perleberg: "We have what we call side-by-side comparisons for new and used cars. People can compare pricing and features of several vehicles at once. They can also compare new versus used and see how that can potentially save hundreds or thousands of dollars. We also focus heavily on helping the consumer make the leasing-versus-buying decision, plus get the most of their trade-in."

Speaking of trade-ins, how can someone get the most money possible when trading in their current vehicle?

Mark Perleberg: "The best thing they can do is get all of the vehicle's paperwork together and organize it. This includes maintenance and repair records. Second, they should have the car thoroughly cleaned and professionally detailed, plus take all of their junk out if it before showing it. You'll be able to get a lot more money on the vehicle if it looks like it's clean and well cared for. Look at your used car from a buyer's perspective. What would you like about it? What would you dislike about it? How could you fix the dislikes before showing that vehicle to a potential buyer? You'll almost always earn more if you were to sell your used car privately.

"The value of a used vehicle is based partly on its condition. Think about what you can do to improve the overall condition of the vehicle to make it more valuable, especially if you'll be selling it privately. The money you earn from the trade-in or sale of your existing car can be put toward the purchase or lease of your new car and help to lower your new monthly payments."

As a former car dealer, what advice do you have for people in terms of working with their salesperson or dealership?

Mark Perleberg: "Figure out what you want to pay and how much you can pay for the vehicle you want. Consider all four major parts of every deal, which are: how much do you want to pay for the car, how much of a down payment can you put down, how much do you want for your trade, and what do you want your monthly payment to be? If you know this information and can convey it to your salesperson, the process of buying or leasing a car will go smoother. The car-buying or -leasing game is not as harsh for the consumer as it used to be. This is mainly because there is not as big of a profit margin for the dealer in each vehicle as there used to be. Thus, it's much harder for a consumer to pay too much for a vehicle.

"It's important to understand that new car dealers especially want to do things the right way and earn the highest customer satisfaction rating possible. You may encounter bad salespeople at a dealer, but in general, dealers in business today want to sell vehicles and generate happy customers. A happy customer will refer new business to that dealer and become a repeat customer down the road, which is extremely important to the dealer's ongoing success. Dealers today have to live with the bad reputation that was created in the 1950s and 1960s. The industry is not at all like it once was.

"Remember that, as the consumer, you always have the ability to simply walk out of a dealership and take your business elsewhere. If you think you're being ripped off or you're being treated poorly, go elsewhere. It's that simple. If you don't like the salesperson helping you, but the dealership has a good reputation, ask to speak with the manager and begin working with a different salesperson. You always have that option as well."

As an automotive journalist, what advice can you offer to consumers about how to get the most out of the car reviews they read?

Mark Perleberg: "I would focus on things in a review that have an impact on you as the driver. Some reviews offer highly technical information that is not important to the average consumer. Other reviews have a very opinionated perspective, based on the reviewer's own ideas and tastes. Reviews can be very helping in offering you other opinions or perspectives about specific vehicles, but ultimately it should be your own test-drive experience that carries the most weight when making a purchase decision. There's no substitute for touching and feeling a car on your own. I personally like cars that go fast and that handle and brake well. I don't mind a bumpier or spongier ride on the freeway, for example. As a consumer, however, you may be looking for a vehicle that offers a very smooth and quiet ride. Reviews can be helpful, because they often focus on new features you might not be aware of."

What are some of the key features new car shoppers should be aware of as they evaluate 2007 and later model year vehicles?

Mark Perleberg: "Gas mileage is a hot topic. I also think resale value is important, because it directly impacts your cost of ownership. If you've narrowed down your vehicle options to three comparable vehicles, for example, check how much value a three-year-old version of each car has retained. You may find that one of those three vehicles will retain its value a lot better than the other two. You might find that all three cars have a MSRP of $25,000 now, but in three years one will likely be worth $15,000 while the other two will only be worth under $10,000. When it comes time to trade in or sell that vehicle, you'll probably want the one with the highest resale value."

Do you have any other advice for car shoppers?

Mark Perleberg: "Never rush the process. Take the time needed to properly shop for a vehicle, test-drive it, and negotiate your best deal. When you're visiting a dealership, leave your kids at home with a babysitter. Be able to focus on the car-buying or -leasing process. Don't expect to visit a dealership during your lunch hour and be able to wrap up the entire process in one quick visit. Also, don't allow the salesperson to rush you into a decision."

More Experts Speak Out

Elsewhere in this book, you'll learn from additional automotive experts who offer advice on hybrid vehicles and how to shop for and choose automotive insurance. The next chapter, however, focuses on how to totally customize and improve your driving experience and the enjoyment of your vehicle by adding manufacturer and dealer-installed options and accessories.

The Dollars and Good Sense of Accessories and Options

WHAT'S IN THIS CHAPTER

- Selecting the most suitable assortment of manufacturer-installed options

- Choosing the dealer-installed options you want and need

- Genuine vs. third-party accessories

- Saving money on accessories and options

f you're shopping for a new vehicle, even after you narrow down your choices to just one, you'll still have many additional decisions to make about the accessories and options you want and need. In addition to offering several versions of each automobile, with various *manufacturer-installed accessories,* all vehicle manufacturers also offer a vast selection of *dealer-installed options* and accessories that allow you to further customize your vehicle and "pimp your ride."

For example, for the 2007 Honda Accord four-door sedan, Honda dealers offer a dozen versions of this popular car, including automatic and manual transmission versions of the Honda Accord VP (Valuable Package), LX, SE (Special Edition), EX, SE V-6, LX V-6, and EX-L V-6. Each of these configurations offers a slightly different selection of manufacturer-installed options and accessories, plus different trim and exterior color options. Of course, each version of the Accord also has a different MSRP, based on the vehicle configuration.

CAR SPEAK   **MANUFACTURER-INSTALLED OPTIONS**—These are extras that the manufacturer installs in a vehicle before shipping it to the dealership. This includes such things as air conditioning, automatic transmission, anti-lock brake systems (ABS), leather seats, power windows, power locks, and exterior/interior color combinations.

DEALER-INSTALLED ACCESSORIES—These are extras that a vehicle buyer selects at the time of purchase and the dealership then professionally installs using genuine products from the vehicle manufacturer. Examples of dealer-installed options include a luggage or bike rack, alloy wheels, floor

---

mats, upgraded stereo systems (including satellite radio), a DVD video system, anti-theft alarm system, fog lights, and a wide range of exterior items to customize the look of the vehicle.

After choosing which vehicle configuration is right for you and after negotiating your best price on that vehicle with your dealer, you can begin looking at the array of dealer-installed options available for that vehicle. Dealer-installed accessories are specific to make, model, and year. So, an accessory available for the 2006 Toyota RAV4, for example, may not be available for the 2007 or 2008 models.

Most manufacturers publish a full-color catalog of dealer-installed options that are available for each vehicle. These options include premium audio systems, GPS navigation systems, bicycle racks, floor mats, steering wheel covers, splash guards, and dozens of other accessories that can be added to a vehicle and professionally installed by the dealership.

Driving Smart

GET WHAT YOU NEED Focus first only on the accessories and options you absolutely need to improve your driving experience. Then, focus on what you can add to the vehicle to improve its look or that you'd enjoy having as a matter of convenience.

LOOK FOR DISCOUNTS Virtually all dealerships will offer a discount of 10 to 25 percent on manufacturer- and dealer-installed accessories you choose when you purchase your vehicle, so negotiate. Some dealers will offer free installation on accessories they install or a discount on the purchase price of each accessory.

Options always add to the price. By the time consumers are done selecting options and accessories, the price of their vehicle has typically risen by hundreds, sometimes thousands of dollars.

Driving Smart

BEFORE OR AFTER? If you purchase dealer-installed accessories when you purchase your vehicle and you're financing it, the cost of the accessories can be added to the amount of your car loan, so you can pay for them over time. Every $1,000 worth of accessories you add to the vehicle will increase your monthly payment by around $20, depending on the term of the loan and your interest rate. If you wait to have the dealer install accessories, you'll have to pay for those accessories and installation in full when you add them.

Selecting the Most Suitable Manufacturer-Installed Options

Every vehicle manufacturer offers a variety of options and accessories that it can install. These tend to be the more costly items that a dealership could not install easily or quickly, such as an automatic transmission, air conditioning, anti-lock brake systems, leather seats, four-wheel drive, or alloy wheels. To make it easier to decide on options, most manufacturers combine as package deals the options that their research shows to be the most popular, typically at a discount from the price of purchasing each option separately.

As you begin shopping around for your ideal vehicle, think about what manufacturer-installed options you absolutely need or want. As you shop around for similar vehicles from different manufacturers, you'll find that some options cost extra in one vehicle but come standard in an otherwise comparable vehicle from another manufacturer. Thus, for each vehicle make and model you're evaluating, it's important to determine which options come standard and which will cost extra.

Create a checklist of the options and accessories that are most important to you in your new vehicle. Bring this checklist to the dealerships and keep it handy when you're doing research online. The following is a checklist of popular options and accessories to help you start your list. (Not all of these options and accessories are available for all vehicles; also, other options and accessories may be available for the vehicles you're considering.)

- Anti-theft alarm or device, such as LoJack (*www.lojack.com*)
- Air conditioning
- Alloy wheels
- All-wheel drive (AWD)
- Anti-lock braking system (ABS)
- Bluetooth handsfree phone system
- Cruise control
- Dual- or tri-zone climate control
- DVD video system
- Foldable/removable backseat(s)
- Front and side airbags
- GPS navigation system (in the dashboard)

- Heated/cooling cup holders
- Heated front seats
- In-dash CD changer
- Leather seats
- Power seats
- Power windows/locks
- Rear-wheel drive
- Rearview camera
- Remote (keyless) entry system
- Sunroof/moon roof
- Surround-sound speakers
- V-6 or V-8 engine
- Other: _____
- Other: _____
- Other: _____
- Other: _____
- Other: _____

When a dealership has new vehicles on the lot and ready to sell, some will have certain options and accessories already installed. This is an ideal situation for the consumer to negotiate the purchase price of those vehicles, because many dealerships will discount the cost of those accessories in order to quickly sell the cars in inventory.

Keep in mind that accessories and options often have two prices—purchase and installation. You can often negotiate the price of either or both prices for each accessory, especially if you're purchasing them when you're purchasing your vehicle.

The best way to know which manufacturer-installed options are available for each make and model, which come standard (included in the base price), and which are considered optional is to visit each manufacturer's Web site. Many of the new car buying directories and car-related Web sites also offer this information in a clear and concise way. Many also allow you to quickly compare two or more vehicles side by side, so you can evaluate them feature by feature as well as by price. (You'll find information about shopping for a vehicle online in Chapter 7.)

Driving Smart

FEATURE BY FEATURE When comparing similar vehicles from different manufacturers or different models from the same manufacturer, do it feature by feature, based on what's included. If the base prices of two vehicles are virtually identical, but air conditioning, for example, is included in one vehicle and would cost $1,500 to add to the other, those two prices are no longer similar. As the saying goes, compare apples to apples and oranges to oranges when it comes to comparing cars, prices, and features.

Buying thousands of dollars in options to "trick out" your vehicle won't typically add to its resale value. Certain options—such as air conditioning, anti-lock brakes, automatic transmission, leather upholstery, and a remote-entry/alarm system—help maintain a vehicle's resale value, but most decorative options, such as fancy trim packages, won't help maintain the value of a vehicle over time or increase the car's resale value.

Driving Smart

ACCESSORIES VS. RESALE Adding thousands of dollars in accessories and options (especially those that are decorative, rather than functional) typically does *not* increase the resale value of the vehicle, nor does it typically help to increase the residual value of a vehicle over time. After 36 months, most vehicles will have a residual value of less than 50 percent of the purchase price. After 60 months, that residual value goes down to below 40 percent of the purchase price, regardless of the accessories and options. In other words, if you spend $1,000 to upgrade to leather seats and $1,000 to upgrade the stereo system and add a DVD video system, don't expect to recoup that money when you resell the vehicle. Focus only on options and accessories you want and need and will use while you own the vehicle.

Choosing the Dealer-Installed Options You Want and Need

The good news about genuine, dealer-installed accessories for a vehicle is that you can have them installed anytime. You can purchase your vehicle, drive it around for a while, and then decide to add a roof rack, a bike rack, a trailer hitch, a cargo organizer, interior or exterior décor, splash guards, or a better audio system, as you discover what you need.

Consider functionality, need, and price. For example, custom-fitted carpet or all-season floor mats add to the décor of the vehicle's interior and serve an important function—to protect the floor from dirt, spills, and other damage. Floor mats or seat covers, for example, serve a dual purpose and can be an excellent investment. You don't, however, have to purchase genuine floor mats or seat covers from the vehicle's manufacturer. You can purchase less expensive floor mats from a third party, as long as they fit your vehicle.

Based on your driving habits and needs, think about what dealer-installed options you need right away, when you purchase your vehicle. If you're not sure a specific accessory is actually needed, hold off for a while and consider adding it later. The questions to ask yourself *before* purchasing each accessory include the following:

- What benefit or functionality does the accessory offer you?
- How will it improve your driving experience, comfort, and/or enjoyment of the vehicle?
- Can you afford the accessory?
- How often will you use the accessory? Will your use make it a good value? If you're considering a bike rack, how often will you be transporting a bicycle? If you're considering fog lights, how often will you be driving at night, in dense fog? If your answer is "Not often," you probably don't need these accessories, so save your money or add to the down payment for the vehicle.
- Instead of purchasing a costly genuine dealer-installed accessory, is there a less expensive but compatible third-party product available?
- Will the accessory save you money over the long term? An alarm system, for example, will typically allow you to qualify for a reduction in your car insurance premiums for the life of the vehicle.

- Does the accessory improve the safety of the vehicle for the driver and/or passengers?
- Will the accessory improve the vehicle's performance or reduce the need for costly repairs?

If you determine that the accessory you're considering will only make the car look better, is something you won't actually use, or won't provide ample benefit to you, don't get it. The vehicles on display in a dealership's showroom often are loaded with accessories. Make sure that you understand what features and options come with the vehicle for its base price (MSRP) and what will cost you extra. The *Monroney sticker*, which federal law requires on the window of every new vehicle for sale, will list the base price, the options

Driving Smart

KEEP A COOL HEAD Don't get caught up in the excitement of buying a new car and wind up adding expensive options you don't really want or need. Ask yourself if you can justify the added expense of each accessory. Do you need a roof rack, for example? How often in the past would you have used one? How much do you anticipate needing one in the future? It's probably not worth it if you'd use the roof rack only once a year to transport luggage on a family road trip or to bring a Christmas tree home. Or those fog lights: they serve a purpose and maybe improve the look of the vehicle, but how often do you drive at night in dense fog? Dealer-installed accessories are very profitable for dealerships. Don't allow the dealer to sell you any accessory that you don't need, even if it adds only a few dollars to your monthly payment.

installed (at the factory or at the dealership), the cost of each option, and the total cost of all the options.

A tricked-out 2007 Honda Element, for example, with the optional side steps, rocker panel trim, roof rack, 16-inch alloy wheels, door visors, splash guards, chrome exhaust finisher, rear bumper guard, rear air deflector, and fog lights looks very different from a basic Element. To add all of these listed decorative features (some of which also serve a purpose) would add more than $3,000 to the vehicle's price.

Genuine vs. Third-Party Accessories

Your new car dealership will typically sell only genuine parts, from the vehicle's manufacturer. The benefit to this is that all of the accessories and options you choose will be installed professionally and have been manufactured specifically for your vehicle based on its model and year. "Genuine" parts and accessories will also perfectly match your vehicle's interior and/or exterior and be covered by a warranty that your dealer will support. For these benefits, however, you will pay a premium.

Depending on the make, model, and year of your vehicle, you can often find compatible accessories manufactured by third parties that cost a fraction of what genuine accessories would cost. While you may save money on the purchase of these accessories, you still often need to have them installed professionally (for a fee). You also have to make sure that installing a specific third-party accessory won't impact the manufacturer's warranty for your vehicle.

You can shop for generic parts and accessories from automotive supply stores in your community or via the Internet. For installation, you can turn to a local mechanic, if the source where you purchase the accessory does not provide installation services. If you're shopping for general car accessories, use any online search engine (such as Google or Yahoo!) and enter the search phrase "car accessories" or "vehicle accessories." If you're looking for a specific accessory, you can make your search phrase more specific, such as "Honda Element accessories" or "Honda Element bike rack."

In addition to retailers and Web sites, also shop for competitive prices using online auction sites, such as eBay (*www.ebay.com*), and/or price-comparison Web sites, such as NexTag.com (*www.nexttag.com*), Shopzilla (*www.shopzilla.com*), PriceSCAN (*www.pricescan.com*), or Pricewatch (*www.pricewatch.com*). Through these price-comparison Web sites, you can find genuine as well as third-party parts and accessories at deeply discounted prices.

Using Nextag.com, for example, you can find a company called Accessories-Honda.com, which offers genuine 2006 Honda Element fog lights, which have a suggested retail price of $348 (excluding installation), being sold for $225 (excluding installation). Best of all, you can save this money simply by spending under three to five minutes doing online research. Similar savings can be found for virtually any accessory, for any make, model, and year of vehicle.

Driving Smart

WATCH YOUR THIRD-PARTY PURCHASES When shopping for third-party accessories, including anything from floor mats to wiper blades or roof racks, make sure what you purchase is designed to fit the specific make, model, and year of your vehicle, and that installing it will not void the manufacturer's warranty for your vehicle.

AFTER-MARKET RUST PROOFING? Most vehicles leave the factory with undercoating protection, rustproofing, and fabric protection. Yet, dealers will often try to sell you additional protection packages that sometimes cost hundreds of dollars. If the vehicle needs this added protection in order to stand up to normal usage and weather, you probably should be looking at a better-quality vehicle. Don't spend money on vehicle protection you don't need, especially since most vehicles are already protected against problems like rust through the manufacturer's warranty.

Entertainment on Wheels

Years ago, vehicles came with an AM/FM radio. If you wanted to spend a bit extra, you could upgrade to a cassette player or a CD player. Now it's possible to upgrade your vehicle's audio system and transform it into a state-of-the-art entertainment center. For example, you can add six, eight, or even ten speakers and a subwoofer to create a true surround-sound experience. You can also get a multi-disc CD changer, a satellite radio receiver, a digital radio receiver, a DVD player, a video game system, an MP3 player, a GPS navigation system, and hands-free cellular phone (Bluetooth) functionality.

Virtually all new cars now can come with a satellite radio receiver, capable of obtaining programming from XM Radio (*www.xmradio.com*) or Sirius Radio (*www.sirius.com*). For a monthly fee, these satellite radio receivers will bring you literally hundreds of commercial-free channels anywhere from coast to coast. Satellite radio also offers specialty-programming stations covering all areas of interest—talk radio, comedy, children's programs, sports, and on and on.

If you want to upgrade your vehicle's audio/video system, first decide what you and your passengers will want and need and then find out what's available that will provide it. Visit consumer electronics retailers (such as Best Buy or Circuit City) to experience the latest in automotive entertainment technology. What you can purchase from well-known third-party companies is often more advanced and provides more choices than what the vehicle manufacturers offer in their standard systems.

Driving Smart

DRIVING WITH KIDS If you spend a lot of time in the car with your kids, a backseat audio/video system capable of playing DVDs or video games will help to keep your kids entertained, especially on long road trips or in traffic. Allowing your kids to enjoy music and movies is far better than hearing them complain and continuously ask, "When are we gonna get there? I'm bored!"

iPOD CONNECTIONS Many of the newer vehicles allow you to quickly attach your Apple iPod or MP3 player to your vehicle's audio system. For information about how to do this, visit the Apple.com Web site to determine what cables and accessories you'll need.

Find Your Way with a GPS Navigation System

Many vehicles now come equipped with a GPS navigation system. If the base model of the vehicle you choose doesn't offer this as a standard feature, you can order one as an option. A less expensive option is to purchase a portable GPS navigation system that can be mounted on your vehicle's dashboard.

For between $400 and $1,000, companies like Magellan (*www.magellangps.com*), TomTom (*www.tomtom.com*), and Garmin (*www.garmin.com*) offer a wide range of portable, high-tech GPS navigation systems that also serve as MP3 players and video monitors. These systems provide detailed maps, turn-by-turn driving directions anywhere in the U.S. (as well as in other countries), and even traffic and weather reports. The prices of these units continue to drop, while the size of the units decreases, but the functionality improves.

The voice prompts and turn-by-turn directions offered by these GPS units makes reading traditional maps or stopping to ask for directions from strangers a thing of the past. If you encounter traffic, road construction, or other delays, a navigation system can instantly propose an alternate route.

Driving Smart

DO YOU NEED NAVIGATION? You can find GPS navigation systems on display at popular consumer electronics retail stores (such as Best Buy, Radio Shack, and Circuit City). Shop around for a system that offers the features you want at a price you can afford.

Be Sure to Protect Your Investment

Now that you've selected your vehicle and picked all of the options and accessories you want and need, the next step is to insure your vehicle and yourself. The next chapter offers information about obtaining the right coverage without overspending.

Having ample insurance coverage can mean the difference between financial security and bankruptcy if you become involved in an automobile accident that results in costly damage, medical bills, and/or lawsuits. As you're about to discover, no matter how much money you have or how well you drive, adequate insurance is an absolute must for all vehicle owners.

CHAPTER 10

Protect Yourself and Your Investment with Insurance

WHAT'S IN THIS CHAPTER

- Vehicle insurance: types and benefits
- Shopping for insurance
- How your annual insurance premium is calculated
- Interview with automotive insurance expert Chris Cunniff of Liberty Mutual Insurance Company

Regardless of where you live or what type of vehicle you drive, you'll need insurance for yourself and for your vehicle. State minimum requirements vary. However, it's essential that when calculating your overall budget and your car-related expenses you include your annual *automobile insurance* premium.

As you'll discover, the more you know about your insurance needs and the more time you invest shopping for the best deals, the more money you can save. This chapter focuses on automotive insurance. It offers strategies for obtaining the types and levels of coverage you want and need from a reliable and highly-rated insurance company. It also offers tips for saving money on your annual insurance premiums.

CAR SPEAK **AUTOMOBILE INSURANCE**–This is insurance that protects against losses involving motor vehicles. The basic types of coverage are bodily injury liability, property damage liability, medical payments or personal injury protection, collision, comprehensive physical damage, and uninsured or underinsured motorist.

Auto insurance offers financial compensation if you become involved in an automobile accident. When you purchase auto insurance, it typically covers you and your spouse, relatives who live in your home, and other licensed drivers who have permission to drive your insured vehicle. There are six basic types of coverage:

- **Bodily Injury Liability.** If your vehicle is involved in an accident that causes injury or death, this coverage pays your legal defense costs and claims against you or family members living with you and others driving your vehicle with your permission.

- **Property Damage Liability.** If your vehicle damages another's property, this coverage pays your legal defense costs and claims against you or family members living with you and others driving your vehicle with your permission, but not the cost of damages to your property, including your vehicle.

- **Medical Payments or Personal Injury Protection.** If your vehicle is involved in an accident, this coverage pays medical expenses and possibly other expenses (such as lost earnings, rehabilitation, replacement of services, and funeral expenses, depending on the policy) for you or any passengers in your vehicle. It also pays medical expenses and possibly other expenses for you or family members injured or killed while riding in another vehicle or injured by another vehicle while walking.

- **Collision.** If your vehicle is involved in a collision with another vehicle or any other object or in a rollover, this coverage pays for damages to your vehicle, regardless of who is responsible.

- **Comprehensive Physical Damage.** If your vehicle suffers damages from theft, fire, hail, wind, flood, vandalism, falling objects, or various other causes (excluding collision or upset), this coverage pays for losses.

- **Uninsured or Underinsured Motorist.** If an uninsured, underinsured, or hit-and-run driver causes property damage or injuries to you or family members and other passengers in your vehicle, this coverage pays for any resulting costs.

Every insurance policy sets a maximum for coverage, a dollar amount per person or per incident, depending on the type of coverage and the situation.

Later in this chapter, you'll learn more about how your insurance company will calculate your *annual premium*. It's based on the level of coverage, types of coverage, *deductibles*, and other criteria.

Driving Smart

READ YOUR POLICY All insurance policies are different. Be sure to check with your insurance company and read your policy to confirm exactly who is covered and to what extent—before you allow others to drive your vehicle.

 CAR SPEAK **ANNUAL PREMIUM**—This is the total price for insurance coverage for a specified period of time (typically one year). This premium can often be divided into monthly payments to make it more affordable.

DEDUCTIBLE—This is the amount the holder of the insurance policy must pay out-of-pocket before the insurance company pays the remainder of a covered loss, up to the specified coverage limits. A deductible can be anywhere from zero to $1,500 or higher. The lower the deductible, the higher the annual premium.

Buy or Lease a Car Without Getting Taken for a Ride

State laws require a minimum level of liability insurance and some states require additional types. Whatever your state requires, it's smart to carry all types and at higher levels of coverage than the required minimums to protect your financial interests and assets. Adequate coverage will generally save you from paying medical expenses, repair costs, and legal judgments and bills that could add up to hundreds of thousands or even millions of dollars, depending on the severity of the accident.

Automotive insurance protects you, your passengers, your vehicle, and your property, and it provides peace of mind. It could keep you out of serious debt and even bankruptcy. Investing the time to work with your insurance agent to make sure you have sufficient coverage is extremely important. The amount of coverage you need and want (beyond any legal requirements) will depend on your personal situation, risk tolerance, and ability and willingness to pay higher premiums for more extensive coverage and higher coverage limits.

If you're leasing a vehicle, you'll still need to maintain insurance. The leasing company will typically require you to possess gap insurance, as well as other types of coverage. If you total the vehicle (as a result of an accident, it can no longer be driven), there may be a difference between the market value of the vehicle and what you still owe on your lease. Gap coverage pays this difference.

> **CAR SPEAK** **GAP INSURANCE**—This is a policy on a leased vehicle that covers the policyholder's termination liability under the lease contract if the vehicle is deemed a complete loss before the end of the lease term. It covers the difference between what the lessee owes and the value of the vehicle at the time of the loss. Gap insurance is typically associated with vehicles that are totaled or stolen. Also known as *gap coverage* or *gap protection*.

Shopping for Automotive Insurance

In addition to finding a policy that provides the coverage you want for a reasonable price, you want to make sure the insurance company is reputable, reliable, and highly rated. All insurance companies are rated by independent companies, such as A.M. Best (*www.ambest.com*) and J.D. Powers and Associates (*www.jdpower.com/finance/ratings/auto_insurance/index.asp*), based on their financial strengths, customer service, and ability to pay claims. An insurance company rated "A++" is the best. The lowest rating available is a "D." For your own protection, only consider working with an insurance company with a rating of "B+" or higher.

When evaluating an insurance company, the level of customer service by telephone, in person, and on the Internet is important. Is someone available to answer your questions or help you to file a claim 24 hours a day, seven days a week? What is the company's average response time once a claim is filed?

One way to learn about an insurance company is to visit your state's department of insurance. You can find out contact information for that agency and your state's auto liability minimum limits on the I-CAN Web site, at *www.ican2000.com/ state.html*.

Don't rely on catchy advertising slogans, cute corporate icons, or multimillion-dollar advertising campaigns to determine if a company is reliable.

Driving Smart

INCREASING DEDUCTIBLES One way to save money on your annual insurance premium is to increase your deductibles. However, that increases your financial risk. If you have a deductible of $1,000 or higher, will you be able to come up with that money if you're involved in an accident? You may be better off paying a higher premium for more peace of mind and financial security. Your decision to go with higher deductibles should be based on your comfort level with risk and your financial situation.

To find the best insurance deal, determine what you actually need (the coverage your state requires) and what you want to protect your financial interests and assets and peace of mind. You'll probably want more extensive coverage than your state requires.

Once you decide on coverage, check with several insurance companies to find the best rates for that coverage. You can contact the insurance companies directly, work with a broker or agent, or use an online insurance quote service.

Online Insurance Quote Services

By completing one online questionnaire, you can obtain insurance quotes from multiple insurance agencies. Here are some of the insurance quote services available on the Internet:

- Esurance.com—*www.esurance.com*
- Ensurance.com—*www.instantcarinsurance.com*
- InsureOne—*www.insureone.com*
- InsWeb—*www.insweb.com*
- LowerMyBills.com (Experian)—*www.lowermybills.com*
- NetQuote—*www.netquote.com*
- Yahoo! Finance Auto Insurance Center—
  finance.yahoo.com/insurance/auto

Driving Smart

AAA INSURANCE If you're a member of the American Automobile Association (AAA), one benefit is discounts on automotive insurance through participating insurance companies. You can obtain price quotes from participating companies from the AAA Web site (*www.aaa.com*) or by calling (800) 222-4242. AAA membership is required.

Contact Insurance Companies Directly

Obtaining an accurate and reliable quote will require you to complete a somewhat detailed questionnaire, so plan on spending about 20 to 30 minutes on the phone, in person, or on a Web site answering questions. If you contact each company individually, you'll need to answer each company's questions. However, if you work with each insurance company individually, you're more likely to save money and get more personalized service.

These are some of the popular automotive insurance companies in the United States:

- Amica Mutual—(800) 242-6422 / *www.amica.com*
- American International Group (AIG) Insurance—(877) 638-4244, *www.aig.com*
- Allstate Auto Insurance—(866) 621-6900, *www.allstate.com*
- GEICO Car Insurance—(800) 861-8380, *www.geico.com*
- Liberty Mutual Insurance—(800) 837-5254, *www.liberty-mutual.com*
- MetLife—(800) MET-AUTO (638-2886), *www.metlife.com*
- Nationwide Insurance—(877) ON-YOUR-SIDE (669-6877), *www.nationwide.com/nw/auto*
- Progressive Auto Insurance—(800) PROGRESSIVE (776-4737), *www.progressive.com*
- State Farm Insurance—*www.statefarm.com/insurance/auto_insurance/auto_insurance.asp*

Driving Smart

J.D. POWER To see how these and other poplar auto insurance companies are rated by J.D. Powers and Associates, visit *www.jdpower.com/finance/ratings/auto_insurance*.

Driving Smart

SIDE BY SIDE After you've obtained quotes from several insurance companies, compare them side by side. Make sure you compare policies that are offering the identical amounts or levels of coverage. Pay attention to the deductibles and policy limits relative to the premiums.

How Your Insurance Premium Is Calculated

Every automotive insurance policy is created specifically for one policyholder based on his or her needs, wants, and ability and willingness to pay the premiums. An insurance company considers a lot of criteria when calculating your annual premium. These criteria vary by state, insurance company, and driver. Here's a comprehensive sampling of what will probably be considered:

- **How much you drive.** The more you're on the road, the greater your chances of an accident. Thus, insurance rates are slightly higher for people who put higher-than-average mileage on their vehicles (more than 15,000 or so miles per year).

- **Driving record.** If you have no moving violations (such as speeding tickets) and no accidents on your record for at least the past three years, you'll typically qualify for a lower premium.

TIP: Before approving your application for auto insurance, an insurance company will obtain a Comprehensive Loss Underwriting Exchange (C.L.U.E.) Report on you, which discloses any and all insurance claims you've made in the past five years. You can obtain a copy of your report for $9.00 by contacting the ChoicePoint Consumer Service Center at (800) 456-6004. You can also order a report through the ChoiceTrust Asset Company Web site, *www.choicetrust.com*. The information on this report will be a factor in calculating your annual premium. The insurance company will also review a copy of your driving record, obtained from your state's Department of Motor Vehicles or Registry of Motor Vehicles.

- **Make and model of vehicle you drive.** Its value, safety record, and popularity among car thieves are all taken into account by the insurance company. Safer cars that are not commonly stolen and that are less expensive to repair are cheaper to insure. If your vehicle is equipped with an alarm or an anti-theft device, this will entitle you to a discount on your premium.

- **Where you live.** Your city or town and state also factor into the calculation of your premium.

- **Your age, sex, and marital status.** Young drivers and senior citizens typically have to pay a slightly higher premium. Some insurance companies also set rates based on sex and marital status.

- **Desired deductibles.** Lower deductibles will raise your premiums and higher deductibles will lower your premiums.

- **Job.** If your job requires a lot of driving, insurance companies will probably charge more.

- **Selected level and type of coverage.** You'll pay more for each type of coverage you select, based on the amount of coverage (policy limit) and the deductible. Some of the common types of coverage include:
  - Liability Coverage - Bodily Injury
  - Liability Coverage - Property Damage (Collision and Comprehensive)
  - Supplementary Coverage
  - Umbrella Liability Coverage
  - Rental Car Coverage (Substitute Transportation)
  - Uninsured/Underinsured Motorist
  - No-Fault Insurance
  - Physical Damage
  - Emergency Road Service
- **Discounts.** Most insurance companies offer discounts to drivers for various reasons. Be sure to ask if you qualify for any. Some discounts will reduce your annual premium by 10 to 20 percent. Depending on the insurance company, there may be discounts for good drivers (no moving violations or accidents for a specified number of years), high school or college students with an average of "B" or higher, drivers who complete a certified driver's education program, people who insure multiple vehicles simultaneously, people who own or lease vehicles with safety equipment (such as anti-lock brakes or anti-theft systems), people who drive less than a specified number of miles per year, people who carpool to commute, and non-smokers.

BODILY INJURY LIABILITY–This insurance coverage pays *CAR SPEAK* your legal defense costs and claims against you or family members living with you and others driving your vehicle with your permission if your vehicle is involved in an accident that causes injury or death. This type of insurance is sold in increments, such as $100,000/$400,000. This means that each of the people you injure could be compensated up to $100,000, but the policy will only cover a maximum of $400,000 per accident.

COLLISION–This insurance coverage pays for damages to your vehicle if your vehicle is involved in a collision with another vehicle or any other object or in a rollover, regardless of who is responsible.

COMPREHENSIVE PHYSICAL DAMAGE–This insurance coverage pays for losses if your vehicle suffers damages from theft, fire, hail, wind, flood, vandalism, falling objects, or various other causes (excluding collision or upset).

MEDICAL PAYMENTS OR PERSONAL INJURY PROTECTION–This insurance coverage pays medical expenses and possibly other expenses (such as lost earnings, rehabilitation, replacement of services, and funeral expenses, depending on the policy) for you or any passengers in your vehicle if your vehicle is involved in an accident and pays medical expenses and possibly other expenses for you or family members injured or killed while riding in another vehicle or injured by another vehicle while walking.

PROPERTY DAMAGE LIABILITY–This insurance coverage pays your legal defense costs and claims against you or family members living with you and others driving your vehicle with your permission, but not the cost of damages to your property, including your vehicle, if your vehicle damages another's property.

> **UNINSURED OR UNDERINSURED MOTORIST**—This insurance coverage pays for any resulting costs if an uninsured, underinsured, or hit-and-run driver causes property damage or injuries to you or family members and other passengers in your vehicle.

Driving Smart

PAY IN ADVANCE You can save on your annual automotive insurance by paying the entire premium in advance. Many insurance companies charge extra if you opt for monthly installments. You can also often save if you have more than one policy with an insurance company, such as homeowner's and automotive insurance.

CREDIT SCORE AND PREMIUMS When you apply for insurance, many companies will obtain a copy of your credit reports and credit scores from the major credit bureaus to help determine if you're a good risk. A low credit score could keep you from obtaining coverage or dramatically increase your premiums. See Chapter 2 for more information about improving your credit score.

Meet Automotive Insurance Expert Chris Cunniff

Chris Cunniff is vice president and product manager of automotive insurance at Liberty Mutual Insurance Company (*www.libertymutual.com*), one of the country's leading insurance companies, with revenues of over $20 billion. Liberty Mutual offers auto insurance, along with other types of insurance, to consumers in all 50 states and other countries. In this interview Cunniff offers advice on how to shop for automotive insurance and save money.

What is the best way for a consumer to choose an auto insurance company?

Chris Cunniff: "There are a number of factors to consider. The price, coverage, and options being offered are all important. The ease of doing business with the insurance company is also worth considering. Can you interact with the company in person, over the telephone, and/or via the Internet? Can you reach the customer service department or file a claim only during business hours or 24 hours per day, seven days a week? Different customers have different preferences about how they like to interact with the companies they do business with. At Liberty Mutual, someone will get the same insurance rates no matter how they choose to interact with us. Different companies, however, may work differently.

"I also recommend looking at an insurance company's overall customer satisfaction rating and the financial strength of the company. I would only consider working with an insurance company that has an 'A' or higher rating from an independent agency, such as A.M. Best."

There are Web sites that allow people to get quotes from multiple insurance companies at once. Do you recommend using such sites or should people contact each insurance company directly?

Chris Cunniff: "A lot of insurance companies, including Liberty Mutual, participate on some of those Web sites, so you can typically get good rate quotes from them. Not all companies, however, participate with each of the insurance quote services."

When people start shopping for automotive insurance, what type of coverage should they get?

Chris Cunniff: "That depends on the individual and their circumstances. The first thing that you need to do is satisfy the minimum insurance requirements for the state where you live. Every state is different. In most states, you're required to have insurance that covers at least $20,000 per accident. That said, most people want to protect their legal assets, so they purchase more than the minimum amount of liability insurance, often up to $100,000 per accident. A homeowner should maintain at least $100,000 worth of coverage. People also need to insure their vehicle, which means they need physical damage coverage. This will help them to repair or replace the car if it's damaged or stolen.

"Uninsured motorist insurance is useful and something that many consumers opt for. This offers coverage if you're injured in an auto accident by someone who doesn't have insurance or who is underinsured. The big thing to consider is how much coverage you really need to properly protect your assets. One excellent way to protect your assets is to supplement your auto insurance with an umbrella policy, which offers additional coverage up to $1 million or more. Medical payment insurance is another type of coverage many people believe is worth having."

How should someone decide what levels their deductibles should be?

Chris Cunniff: "It depends on a consumer's financial situation and their ability to cover out-of-pocket expenses in the event of an accident. A $250 deductible means that if you're involved in an accident, your out-of-pocket expense would be $250. The insurance company would then cover everything else up to the limit of the policy. Many people opt for a $500 deductible in order to lower their annual premium. You could also select a $1,000 or $1,500 deductible.

"When you purchase insurance, get a few different quotes incorporating several different deductibles. This allows you to evaluate the increase in premium vs. the reduction of the deductible. Given that most people are involved in an auto accident only once every 10 years, you might not want to pay $200 or so extra per year for a $250 deductible, and settle for a less costly $500 deductible, for example."

Is there an easy way to determine if you have ample coverage?

Chris Cunniff: "In terms of determining if you have adequate coverage, I recommend sitting down with a licensed insurance agent who will be able to go over your personal needs, review your existing policy, and help you select adequate coverage levels. Most insurance companies will insure based on actual cash value. I recommend if you're driving a new vehicle that you choose new vehicle replacement coverage."

What are some of the things that an insurance company considers when setting the annual premium for auto insurance?

Chris Cunniff: "The number-one thing is someone's driving record. Someone with a clean record, meaning no accidents or moving violations, will get a much better rate than someone with a not-so-clean driving record. Beyond someone's driving record, different insurance companies use different criteria to determine what to charge. In general, higher coverage levels cost more, but you can balance this by selecting higher deductibles, which will lower your annual premiums.

"The vehicle you drive also determines your insurance premiums, as do the types and amounts of coverage you opt to purchase. If you drive a safe vehicle, which is one that scores well in independently conducted crash tests, this will help keep your premiums down. If, however, you drive a vehicle that's more frequently stolen by car thieves, this will raise your premium. Vehicles, like sports cars, that cost a lot to repair also require us to charge higher premiums.

"Before you buy a new or used vehicle, you can research the safety ratings of a vehicle to help determine whether or not it'll cost you a lot extra to insure it. One resource for researching a vehicle's safety records, based on its make, model, and year, is the Highway Loss Data Institute [*www.hldi.org*]."

Driving Smart

THE SAFEST MODELS The Highway Loss Data Institute and the Insurance Institute for Highway Safety (*www.hldi.org*) annually publish a summary of the current model year's safest vehicles by category. The vehicles are rated as good, acceptable, marginal, or poor based on performance in high-speed front and side crash tests and evaluations of seat and head restraints for protection against neck injuries in rear impacts.

What is the biggest misconception people have about auto insurance?

Chris Cunniff: "People don't realize how much insurance companies pay out in claims compared to how much they earn in premiums. Generally, for every $1.00 we take in, we pay out 95 cents in claims or operating expenses."

What are some ways the average person can save money on their auto insurance?

Chris Cunniff: "Maintaining a clean driving record will help a lot in terms of keeping your premiums as low as possible. You also buy or lease the safest possible vehicle. Also, don't buy a lower deductible than you actually need. If you have money and can afford to pay $1,000 out-of-pocket in the event you're involved in an accident, you don't need to pay extra for a $500 or even a $250 deductible. The insurance companies also offer many different types of discounts which your insurance agent can go over with you to determine which of these discounts you'd qualify for. Many companies will offer a multi-policy discount, for example.

"Liberty Mutual is associated with over 9,000 affinity groups, including corporations, professional associations, credit unions, colleges, and universities, and we offer auto insurance discounts to people associated with these groups, companies, or organizations. Be sure to ask your insurance agent or sales representative about what discounts you qualify for. The savings can be substantial.

"Unless you're able to pay your entire annual premium in one payment, you will pay a monthly billing fee if you opt to pay your premium using monthly or quarterly payments. If you're charged a billing fee of $4 per month, for example, that's $48 per year extra you're paying.

"Based on the other types of insurance coverage you already have, whether it's medical insurance or a homeowner's policy, you may be able to avoid overlapping coverage that you don't need to pay for with your auto insurance. This is something you can determine by sitting down with a licensed insurance agent or sales representative. For example, some people may be paying extra for roadside assistance through their auto insurance, but already be receiving that coverage through their vehicle manufacturer or through a membership with AAA. This is duplicated coverage that could potentially be eliminated."

What are some of the biggest mistakes people make when shopping for auto insurance?

Chris Cunniff: "People focus only on price, instead of the coverage and customer service they're receiving for that price. Also, once you acquire your insurance, if your personal circumstances change, you may want to have your policy reevaluated to make sure you have ample coverage. For example, if you purchase a new home, you add a teenage driver to your policy, or you acquire additional assets you want to protect, you'll probably want to increase your coverage. When you're shopping for insurance, don't be afraid to ask your agent a lot of questions."

Driving Smart

ACCIDENT FORGIVENESS Ask your insurance company if it offers an accident forgiveness program. If so, this can keep your premiums from increasing dramatically if you're involved in an auto accident.

INSURANCE CARD Once you acquire insurance, you will be provided with a proof of insurance card or certificate by your insurance company. You should keep this card or certificate, contact information for your insurance company, and your vehicle title and registration in your vehicle at all times. Also, keep copies of these documents in a safe place at home or at work or in a safety deposit box.

CHAPTER 11

Make a Statement: Drive a Hybrid

WHAT'S IN THIS CHAPTER

- An introduction to hybrid vehicles
- Why drive a hybrid?
- Interview with hybrid vehicle expert Bradley Berman

Buy or Lease a Car Without Getting Taken for a Ride

There's an age-old saying, "Actions speak louder than words." Well, you can go around town shouting from the rooftops how important it is to protect the environment, conserve the planet's natural resources, and be more environmentally friendly—*or* you can take action yourself. One way people are taking a stand and doing something to help protect the environment and conserve fuel is to buy a hybrid vehicle.

Hybrids are now available from many vehicle manufacturers, including Honda, Toyota, Ford, Saturn, GMC, Chevrolet, and Lexus, with new models being introduced each year. The technology behind these vehicles is improving quickly, making them more cost-effective, more powerful, and more fuel-efficient.

HYBRID VEHICLE–This is any vehicle that uses two or more sources of power, typically an electric motor with batteries and a gas- or diesel-powered engine (hybrid electric vehicle, HEV). **CAR SPEAK**

As of early 2007, hybrid vehicles still cost more than conventional vehicles. In fact, even with the fuel savings, it would most likely take you four or five years, maybe longer, to recoup your investment. The primary reasons why people drive hybrids are to make a positive statement about the environment and to contribute to reducing pollution. People who drive hybrids are willing to pay a little more upfront to be able to do so.

If you're interested in making a statement and making a difference, consider purchasing or leasing a hybrid vehicle. If, however, you're hoping that a hybrid will save you money, you'll need to wait a few years for the next generation of hybrid vehicles to hit the market.

This chapter offers a basic introduction to hybrid vehicles. While hybrids certainly have their advantages, they're definitely not a viable option for everyone. So, before you purchase or lease a hybrid vehicle, make sure that the hybrid you choose actually offers the power and functionality you need from a vehicle and that purchasing or leasing a hybrid makes financial sense for you.

Driving Smart

WEB SOURCES One of the most useful resources for learning about hybrid vehicles (from a source that's independent, unbiased, and knowledgeable) is the HybridCars.com Web site (*www.hybridcars.com*). Later in this chapter, you'll read an interview with HybridCars.com founder Bradley Berman, who offers additional information and insight into these vehicles.

FUEL ECONOMY INFO If you're shopping for a vehicle based on fuel economy, there are many traditional, gas-powered vehicles that offer excellent fuel efficiency. The Edmunds.com Web site (*www.edmunds.com*), for example, lists and reviews the most fuel-efficient vehicles for each model year. When fuel efficiency is discussed in the automotive industry, the data used is based on the Environmental Protection Agency's miles-per-gallon ratings for city and highway travel. The FuelEconomy.gov Web site is an excellent resource for learning about the fuel efficiency rating of every make, model, and year of vehicle from 1985 to the present.

An Introduction to Hybrid Vehicles

Hybrids come in a wide range of styles, from two-door compacts to midsize luxury SUVs. In 2005, over 200,000 hybrid vehicles were sold. This represents just 1.2 percent of the 17 million new cars sold that year. It's predicted that by 2010, hybrid sales will increase to between 600,000 and one million vehicles per year.

Before jumping on the hybrid bandwagon, however, there are some basic things you should understand about this evolving technology. For example, if you're thinking of saving the environment and eliminating harmful emissions, you should know that even if everyone were driving hybrids, this would be only a partial solution for the environmental and energy problems facing our planet.

Today's hybrid vehicles that use electric motors do not need to be plugged in. Thanks to a technology known as *regenerative braking*, the batteries recharge as you drive. There's also a popular myth that the batteries in hybrids need to be replaced often and that they're costly. Well, the warranty that comes with most hybrids and covers their batteries is for between 80,000 and 100,000 miles. While there are few reliable statistics on the life of hybrid batteries, most research shows that it's anywhere from 150,000 miles to 200,000 miles and maybe more. After the manufacturer's warranty expires, however, the cost of replacing the battery is typically high.

Who's driving hybrids? Well, in addition to those Hollywood celebrities such as Leonardo DiCaprio and

Cameron Diaz, the Office for the Study of Automotive Transportation at the University of Michigan reports that the average hybrid owner can be described as follows:

- High income (over $100,000 per year)
- Average age: 40s to 50s
- Much more likely to be female than male
- They drive fewer miles per year than typical drivers (less than 15,000 miles)
- They plan to keep their vehicles longer (at least five years)
- They are willing to pay extra for an environmentally friendly vehicle
- They want to do something to help reduce vehicle pollution
- They expect fuel prices to continue to rise

Driving Smart

HOW IT WORKS For a detailed explanation of how hybrids work, visit *auto.howstuffworks.com/hybrid-car.htm*.

Why Drive a Hybrid?

The primary reason to drive a hybrid is to make a statement that you're concerned about the environment. The second reason for driving a hybrid is fuel efficiency. Not all hybrids are designed for fuel efficiency, however. While some hybrids get 35 to 50 miles per gallon, "performance hybrids" tend to get only between 20 and 30 miles per gallon.

When focusing on fuel efficiency, keep in mind that the EPA's estimates tend to be overstated, because they're based on continuous, peak driving conditions. In the real world, achieving the advertised MPGs typically isn't possible— whether you're driving a hybrid or a traditional gas-powered vehicle. Your driving habits will play a huge role in the gas mileage your vehicle achieves.

One reason why some people enjoy driving hybrids is because many of them are packed with standard features for comfort and luxury and with the latest electronic gadgets. Most owners also report they're extremely fun to drive.

As you shop for a hybrid, make sure you understand the state of the technology and your expectations are realistic. For example, one of the drawbacks of early hybrids, limited passenger capacity and stowage space, has been remedied in current hybrid models, but space in some vehicles may be less than you expect.

Driving a hybrid helps to reduce pollution and slow global warming, since hybrids create fewer greenhouse gases. The impact that you, one driver of one hybrid vehicle, will have on the environment is minimal, but you can sleep better knowing you're not damaging the environment like the driver of a ten-year-old, gas-guzzling auto that barely meets emission standards.

The manufacturer's warranties offered with most new hybrids is also impressive. The typical warranty on a new hybrid is for eight years/100,000 miles or ten years/150,000 miles, which is actually better than warranties for many new gas-powered vehicles. Thus, the idea that hybrids have more mechanical problems and are more costly to repair than gas-powered vehicles is generally wrong.

These are some of the benefits associated with driving a new hybrid:

- Lower emissions
- Smoother ride
- Reduced noise
- Longer battery life
- Better fuel economy
- More environmentally responsible

Driving Smart

HYBRID CALCULATORS The HybridCars.com Web site features a calculator to help you quickly compare fuel consumption and related costs between a specific make and model of hybrid and a comparable gas-powered vehicle. Follow this link to calculate gas consumption, fuel cost, and emission of major pollutants: *www.hybridcars.com/calculator.*

HYBRID CITIES According to research conducted by R.L. Polk & Company, the five U.S. cities where hybrid cars were the most popular in 2006 were Los Angeles, San Francisco, New York, Washington, and Boston.

The Cost of Hybrids

One thing to understand about hybrids is that, due to demand, dealers are able to charge the full sticker price for most hybrid models. In some cases, consumers are also forced to pay a dealer markup. For 2007 vehicle models, hybrid vehicles tend to cost about 20 percent more than their traditional gas-powered counterparts. This translates to an additional cost of $2,500 to $3,000 for most low- to mid-priced hybrids. Just as with traditional cars, prices vary greatly, based on the make and model. For example, it's not hard to find a low-end hybrid priced in the low $20,000s, while a more luxurious hybrid costs upwards of $50,000.

As time goes on, technology will improve, demand will increase, and more manufacturers will begin offering hybrid vehicles. Prices are expected to drop in the future, so hybrids will be similar in price to the vehicles they're replacing.

People who drive hybrids now are passionate about their vehicles and willing to pay more, if necessary, to drive them. Over time, the tax credits and the money saved on gas will make up for the difference in the purchase price of a hybrid,

Driving Smart

TAX CREDITS The U.S. government still offers some tax credits for people who purchase and drive certain hybrid vehicles. To learn about tax incentives currently being offered, visit *www.fueleconomy.gov/feg/taxcenter. shtml*. Some tax credits are for several thousand dollars, but some may be for as little as a few hundred dollars, which is why doing advance research is important. The tax credits are slowly being phased out. Hybrid vehicles purchased after December 31, 2010 will not be eligible for any tax credit. Based on how quickly hybrids are being sold, it's conceivable that the tax credits for certain models will not be available after 2007.

but that may take between three and five years and maybe longer. It should be noted that most hybrid vehicles currently on the market maintain very strong resale values.

Driving Smart

INSURANCE DISCOUNTS Some insurance companies offer a five to ten percent discount to hybrid car owners. Contact your insurance agent to find out if a hybrid discount is offered.

Hybrid Vehicle Manufacturers

In the 2006 model year, there were 16 hybrid models available. By 2011, J.D. Powers reports there will be at least 38 hybrid models on the market. To learn about the hybrid models and about features, pricing, and other important information, visit the Web sites of the manufacturers listed below. You can also read reviews of the popular hybrids at the HybridCars.com Web site and on many of the Web sites presented in Chapter 7.

The chart on page 233 is a listing of hybrid models available in 2007 or slated to be introduced in 2008.

Driving Smart

FUEL ECONOMY CHAMPIONS In the 2006 model year, the Honda Civic, Honda Insight, and Toyota Prius were rated as the most fuel-efficient hybrid vehicles.

Buy or Lease a Car Without Getting Taken for a Ride

Manufacturer	Web Site	Hybrid Models Currently Offered (as of 2007)
Chevrolet	www.chevrolet.com	Equinox Hybrid Malibu Hybrid Tahoe Hybrid Silverado Hybrid (2008)
Dodge	www.dodge.com	Ram Durango Two-Mode Hybrid (2008)
Ford	www.ford.com	Escape Hybrid Fusion Hybrid (2008)
GMC	www.gmc.com	Yukon Hybrid Sierra Hybrid (2008)
Honda	www.honda.com	Accord Hybrid Civic Hybrid Insight Hybrid Fit Hybrid (2008)
Lexus	www.lexus.com	GS Hybrid HS Hybrid LS Hybrid
Mercury	www.mercuryvehicles.com	Mariner Hybrid Milan Hybrid (2008)
Nissan	www.nissanusa.com	Nissan Altima Hybrid
Saturn	www.saturn.com	Vue Green Line HybridGreen Line Aura
Toyota	www.toyota.com	Camry Hybrid Highlander Hybrid Prius Sienna Minivan (2008)
Hyundai	www.hyundaiusa.com	Accent Hybrid (2009)
Porsche Cayenne	www.porsche.com/usa	Cayenne (2008)

Driving Smart

MORE COMING Additional hybrids that have been announced, but that as of the publication of this book did not have an official release date, include Cadillac Escalade, Ford Edge, Honda Pilot, Lincoln MKX, Mazda Tribute, Ford 500, Hyundai Sonata, Kia Rio, and Honda Ridgeline.

Interview with Hybrid Vehicle Expert Bradley Berman

For anyone interested in learning more about hybrid vehicles in general or the specific makes and models of hybrid vehicles on the market, one of the best Web sites to visit is definitely HybridCars.com (*www.hybridcars.com*).

Bradley Berman is the editor of HybridCars.com. He also writes about hybrids for *BusinessWeek* and *The New York Times*. In this interview, Berman offers additional insights and advice about hybrids.

What does the HybridCars.com Web site offer?

Bradley Berman: "It's a consumer information Web site that educates the public about hybrid vehicles. I started the Web site in 2002, after purchasing a Honda Civic hybrid. I had a background in Web site publishing, so this seemed like an ideal way to deliver timely and accurate information to the public about these automobiles. Two of my goals are to dispel the many myths about hybrids and to create an online community where hybrid vehicle owners can communicate with each other."

In your opinion, what are some of the best reasons for someone to purchase a hybrid?

Bradley Berman: "The overall best reason to buy one is because they represent the most significant improvement in automotive technology since cars were first introduced over 100 years ago. These cars minimize our impact on the environment, reduce our dependence on gas, plus they're a lot of fun to drive."

How do you define a hybrid vehicle?

Bradley Berman: "It's a vehicle that is powered by more than one source of energy. In the future, there will be much greater diversity in terms of alternate fuel and technology utilized. We're entering an age of energy diversity. Right now, most hybrids on the market are gas-electric hybrids."

What is a performance hybrid vehicle?

Bradley Berman: "People define hybrid vehicles in different ways. A performance hybrid focuses more on power and performance, as opposed to fuel efficiency."

Are hybrid vehicles always cost-effective for the owner?

Bradley Berman: "Not all hybrids offer a return on investment. Some of the best-selling hybrids, like the Prius or Honda Civic, for example, offer a cost savings to the consumer and a faster payback period for recouping the premium cost of the vehicle. Let's be very clear. Cars are a symbol of our personal identity and are a reflection of our values. People buy hybrids and tend to pay extra for them because these vehicles represent something they believe in. These vehicles allow people to showcase their interest in the environment and to help bring about a change in the automotive industry that they'd like to see."

What advice can you offer for someone who might be interested in buying or leasing a hybrid?

Bradley Berman: "First, take a test-drive and experience what these vehicles are like firsthand. See if any of the hybrids currently on the market will satisfy your needs. Some of the hybrids offer cool features, like a very quiet driving experience. You can drive these vehicles just as you world a gas- or diesel-powered vehicle and not have to modify your driving habits in any way. Beyond that, look at the bottom line. If you care about fuel efficiency, research how fuel-efficient the hybrid vehicle you're interested in actually is. Some traditional vehicles are as fuel-efficient as some hybrids."

What are some of the worst mistakes you see people make when shopping for a hybrid?

Bradley Berman: "People buy a hybrid because they want good fuel economy, but their personal driving habits don't allow for maximum fuel efficiency. For example, people drive very fast, carry a lot of heavy cargo, take a lot of very short trips, or don't maintain proper tire pressure. All of these things greatly reduce fuel efficiency in all vehicles, not just hybrids. If you're not going to take advantage of a fuel-efficient vehicle, why bother to drive a hybrid? Make sure you select a vehicle that meets your wants and needs and that is suitable for your driving habits."

What new hybrid technologies or advances should consumers be expecting over the next few years?

Bradley Berman: "Plug-in hybrids are on the horizon. They represent yet another significant technological advancement that will greatly improve the fuel efficiency, power, and the capabilities of hybrid vehicles. These cars will utilize an all-electronic mode for the majority of your driving. Vehicles with this new technology, which favors electricity more than gasoline, will probably be released between 2009 and 2011."

Driving Smart

PLUG-IN HYBRID GM was the major first vehicle manufacturer to announce that it's developing a plug-in hybrid. At a press conference held during the Los Angeles Auto Show on November 20, 2006, Rick Wagoner, GM Chairman and CEO, stated, "GM has begun work on a Saturn Vue plug-in hybrid production vehicle. The technological hurdles are real, but we believe they are also surmountable. I can't give you a production date for our plug-in hybrid today. But I can tell you that this is a top-priority program for GM, given the huge potential it offers for fuel-economy improvement.... We intend to bring our substantial global resources to bear on this issue."

Protect Your Investment and Save Money

Whether you're driving a new car or a used car that's new to you, there are definitely things you can do in your driving in order to protect your vehicle, extend its life, and save money. The next chapter discusses basic car maintenance tips that'll save you money.

Car Maintenance Tips That'll Save You Money

WHAT'S IN THIS CHAPTER

- Ten easy strategies for maintaining your vehicle
- Saving money while taking care of your car
- Avoiding costly repairs
- Choosing a mechanic

O nce you've purchased or leased a vehicle, new or used, you'll probably want to protect your investment and keep it in peak working condition in order to avoid costly repair bills. This chapter presents some easy strategies for maintaining your vehicle and saving money.

Driving Smart

AAA MEMBERSHIP For 24-hour roadside assistance and a range of other services, consider joining AAA. If you break down, run out of gas, lock your keys in your car, or need help planning a road trip, an AAA membership can save you a lot of time, effort, stress, and money. Members can also receive special discounts when shopping for insurance and get help finding reputable mechanics. Membership starts at around $50 a year for a basic membership; however, a premium AAA Plus membership offers significantly greater benefits. Adding family members to your membership will cost about $25 a year per person. For details, call (800) JOIN-AAA (564-6222) or visit the AAA Web site, *www.aaa.com*. Once you're an AAA member, if you ever need roadside assistance at any time, simply dial (800) AAA-HELP (222-4357). Especially if you're buying a used vehicle, an AAA membership is an excellent investment.

Ten Easy Maintenance Tips That'll Save You Money and Aggravation

The following ten maintenance tips will save you money, keep your vehicle operational, and help make your driving experience safer and more enjoyable:

1. **Read the entire owner's manual for your vehicle.** It will contain

Driving Smart

SCHEDULED MAINTENANCE Regularly maintaining your vehicle and following the regular maintenance procedures recommended by the manufacturer will help you achieve maximum fuel efficiency and avoid costly repairs.

important details about your vehicle that will help you easily maintain it and show you how to operate all of its features.

2. **Maintain proper tire pressure.** This is important. It will not only save gas, but also extend the life of the tires and ensure greater safety in all weather conditions. Under normal use, a tire can lose one psi (pound per square inch) of pressure every month. Additionally, for every ten-degree drop in temperature, an additional one psi will be lost. If you're carrying extra weight in your vehicle, such as a lot of luggage or heavy items in your trunk, pay more attention to keeping your tires properly inflated. For under $10, you can buy a tire gauge that you should keep in your glove compartment. If just one tire is underinflated by only ten psi, your fuel economy can decrease by four percent and you'll significantly shorten the life of the tire and put extras wear on your vehicle.

3. **Rotate and balance the tires,** as recommended by the vehicle and/or tire manufacturer. This is typically required every 5,000 to 7,500 miles. Rotating your tires as recommended by the manufacturer will add as much as 10,000 miles to

the life of the tires. As you're having your tires rotated, have them checked for damage or excessive wear. Driving with improperly inflated or damaged tires can be a safety risk.

4. **Change the oil regularly**, based on the manufacturer's recommendations. For older vehicles, an oil change is recommended every 3,000 miles or every three months. Newer vehicles typically require oil changes less frequently. Be sure to use the appropriate type of motor oil in your vehicle.

5. **Take brake noises seriously.** If you step on the brakes and the vehicle pulls to one side, the brake pedal sticks to the floor, you hear a screeching or grinding or scraping sound, or the "brake" warning light on the vehicle's instrument panel comes on, have a brake specialist check your vehicle immediately.

6. **Check all fluids in your vehicle regularly.** Do it at least once per month, more often if your vehicle is older. This includes the antifreeze/coolant, transmission fluid, brake fluid, power steering fluid, windshield washer fluid, and oil. Never overfill any fluid containers in your vehicle. (When you have an oil change, request that all of the vehicle's fluids be checked and topped off as needed.) Failing to replace key fluids will lead to poor engine performance, increase fuel consumption, and eventually cause severe engine damage. While you're checking the fluids, check the belts and hoses for damage.

7. **Keep the air filter clean.** Replace it if it gets very dirty or as part of a regular tune-up. A clogged air filter can increase fuel consumption by ten percent or more.

8. **Replace your windshield wiper blades annually**, more frequently if they're leaving smudges on the windshield.

9. **Have your battery tested every few months.** The lifespan for a car battery is usually three to four years.

10. **Keep the gas tank at least one-quarter full at all times.** This help keep the engine clean and running smoothly, especially in cold weather.

Driving Smart

STRANGE NOISES If your car starts making unusual noises or warning lights go on, don't ignore these symptoms of potential problems. Visit your dealership or a mechanic immediately to have the problem diagnosed and fixed.

Seven More Tips for Saving Money on Gas

The following tips will help keep you save money on gas:

1. Avoid excessive idling or sitting in traffic for extended periods.

2. Avoid using the air conditioner when traveling at slow speeds, but over 40 mph close the windows and use the air conditioner. Open windows cause drag, which reduces fuel efficiency.

3. Don't overfill the gas tank. Tighten the gas cap properly.

4. Remove junk and other heavy items you don't need from

your trunk. If your vehicle has a roof rack, don't leave heavy items on it if you're not using them.

5. Use the grade of fuel recommended by the vehicle manufacturer. With the exception of sports cars, newer vehicles in particular will not benefit from higher-octane (more expensive) fuel, so use the lowest grade recommended by the manufacturer. It does not matter what brand of gas you use.

6. Use cruise control. At 55 mph your fuel economy will typically be 20 percent higher than at 70 mph.

7. Apply for a credit card from your favorite gas station chain. Many of these cards offer significant discounts when you purchase gas. With gas prices between $2.00 and $3.00 per gallon, a three percent rebate can mean a savings of $.06 to $.09 cents per gallon. Small savings add up.

Driving Smart

GAS CREDIT CARD REBATES To find the gas credit cards with the best rebate deals (and apply for those cards), visit *www.creditcardscenter.com/gascards.html*, *www.pumpandsave.com*, *the-best-credit-card.com/gas-rebate-credit-cards*, or *www.indexcreditcards.com/gascreditcards.html*.

Equipping Your Glove Compartment or Trunk

In your vehicle, you should keep some basic tools, first aid gear, and other necessities. The following is a basic checklist of items you'll want to keep in your glove compartment or trunk:

- ❏ A copy of your vehicle registration, proof of insurance, and a photocopy of your driver's license
- ❏ Basic tools (including Phillips and flat-head screwdrivers, socket wrenches, and pliers)
- ❏ Blanket
- ❏ Car charger for your cell phone
- ❏ Electrical tape
- ❏ Emergency warning triangles or beacons
- ❏ First aid kit
- ❏ Flashlight (with extra batteries)
- ❏ Gloves
- ❏ Jumper cables
- ❏ Pad of paper and pen
- ❏ Snowbrush and ice scraper (cold climate)
- ❏ Spare tire and jack
- ❏ Sunglasses
- ❏ Tire pressure gauge

Tips for Choosing a Mechanic

When choosing a mechanic, you want someone who meets the following criteria:

- competitively priced
- experienced
- friendly
- honest
- knowledgeable

- reliable
- well-trained

The very best way to find the perfect mechanic is through word-of-mouth. Get a referral from someone you know and trust, who has used the mechanic and was pleased with the results. Your local authorized dealership is often the place to go for major repairs to your vehicle, because the mechanics have the knowledge, experience, and access to genuine parts. However, you'll discover that not all dealerships are as honest and easy to work with as others, so don't automatically go to the closest dealership if a dealership slightly farther away has a better reputation.

While all vehicle manufacturers certify mechanics to work on specific makes and models of vehicles and provide their own training, most well-trained and reputable mechanics are also independently certified by the National Institute for Automotive Service Excellence (ASE), which is the only national organization that certifies automotive technicians. An ASE technician will typically have an area of expertise in which they've received specialized training, thus making him

NATIONAL INSTITUTE FOR AUTOMOTIVE SERVICE EXCEL- *CAR SPEAK*
LENCE (ASE)—A nonprofit organization that offers comprehensive testing and certification of automotive technicians and mechanics, who then have the right to refer to themselves as ASE Certified Technicians and the responsibility to follow a strict code of ethics. To learn more about this organization or to obtain a local referral, visit the organization's Web site at *www.asecert.org.*

or her, for example, a brake specialist, a transmission specialist, an engine specialist, or an exhaust specialist.

Whether you have your vehicle repaired at a local dealership or you use an independent mechanic, check the credentials of the mechanic or automotive technician. Make sure he or she has experience working on your vehicle (make, model, and year) and access to the necessary parts. Find out about the parts the mechanic will be using. Genuine or third-party? New or reconditioned?

Driving Smart

TRAINING AND TOOLS In addition to finding a mechanic with experience and training, make sure the repair shop is equipped with modern tools and equipment and is clean and well organized, and that the staff treats you professionally and courteously. A reputable mechanic or repair shop will have all prices, policies, and guarantees clearly posted on signs and/or will give you them in writing. Also, look for signs of professionalism, such as a plaque showing membership in the local Better Business Bureau, certifications from the vehicle manufacturer, AAA-Approved Auto Repair status, Blue Seal of Excellence Recognition Program status, and ASE certifications.

Follow these steps for finding and working with a mechanic:

1. Find a reputable, experienced, and well-trained mechanic. You can contact the local Better Business Bureau (*www.bbb.org*) to determine if it's received any complaints about the mechanic you're considering.

2. If you're shopping around for a mechanic, collect written

estimates. Compare labor costs, parts costs, and guarantees that they offer.

3. Have the mechanic diagnose the problem. There may be a fee for this.

4. Obtain a written estimate for the work to be done and an estimate of the time to complete the repair. The estimate should define the problem and list the parts needed and the anticipated labor charges. It should be signed and dated by the mechanic.

5. Make sure the repair shop/mechanic will honor your vehicle's manufacturer's warranty.

6. Find out exactly how much the mechanic will charge for the repair, including all labor and parts. What's the hourly labor rate?

7. Approve the estimate.

8. Have the mechanic complete the repair.

9. Review the work done by the mechanic and take the vehicle for a test-drive.

10. Obtain a written guarantee for the repair.

Driving Smart

FIND A MECHANIC As soon as you acquire a vehicle, start looking for a mechanic. Then, if a problem occurs, you immediately know where to take your vehicle: you won't need to find a mechanic in a hurry or settle on the first mechanic you find. Consider using the same mechanic, if possible, to handle all routine maintenance on your vehicle (oil changes, tire rotations, etc.) and any major repairs.

11. Pay for the repair by credit card, if possible.

12. Keep copies of all service documents.

Communicating About Problems

When you experience a mechanical problem with your vehicle, you might not immediately be able to identify exactly what's wrong, but you should be able to identify the symptoms and discuss them with your mechanic. If a problem occurs, be alert to strange sounds (squeals, clicks, rumbles, grinding noises, screeches, etc.), vibrations, drips, leaks, smells, smoke, warning lights, and gauge readings. You may also notice a difference in your vehicle's acceleration or braking, a loss of engine performance, or a dramatic reduction in fuel economy.

Make a list of all the symptoms for your mechanic and be able to tell him or her whether the problem is constant or intermittent. If the problem is intermittent, when does it happen? For example, does the problem occur only when you're accelerating or braking, when you're shifting, or just when the engine is cold? Also, when did the problem start? This is all

---

Driving Smart

KNOW THE SYMPTOMS It's smart to write down all of the symptoms and give a list to your mechanic. This way, you won't forget anything when you drop off the vehicle for service. As you're discussing the situation with your mechanic, ask questions. Make sure you give him or her enough time to diagnose the problem accurately.

---

extremely useful information for your mechanic. Details like these can help him or her diagnose the problem more quickly and accurately.

After a mechanic has diagnosed the problem, before you approve the recommended repairs, make sure you understand all of the repair shop's rates and policies—including hourly labor rates, guarantees, and methods of payment accepted. Also, when you request a written estimate of the work to be done, get an estimate of when the work will be completed. Ask if the shop will provide a free loaner car.

Don't Neglect Routine Maintenance

Every vehicle manufacturer recommends specific maintenance work according to specific mileage points. This information will be listed in the owner's manual for your vehicle and is considered preventive maintenance. If you have this work done at the specified times, you will increase the life of your vehicle, help ensure that it will always run well, and avoid costly repairs. Calculate the costs of these repairs into your budget when selecting your vehicle and then make sure you have the preventive maintenance done as recommended.

Driving Smart

KEEP RECORDS Keep a detailed log or written records of all work on your vehicle and keep copies of receipts. If you decide to sell your vehicle, you may be able to get a higher price if you can provide the paperwork for all routine maintenance done on the vehicle.

In addition to the recommended maintenance work, if you live in an area where the seasons and temperatures change dramatically, it's a good idea to have your car tuned up for the summer and winter. Your dealership or mechanic will be able to suggest what should be done to the vehicle to prepare it for extremely hot or cold temperatures.

Driving Smart

UNDERSTANDING THE PROBLEM The Automotive Maintenance Repair Association/Motorist Assurance Program (AMRA/MAP) has created a simple online guide, *How to Find Your Way Under the Hood and Around the Car*, which includes a maintenance check list. You can find it and other useful vehicle information on the (AMRA/MAP) Web site, at *www.motorist.org/ motorists/motorist.htm*.

Other Books by Jason R. Rich from Entrepreneur Press

The following titles are now available wherever books are sold or can be ordered through the EntrepreneurPress.com Web site. For more information about these and other books written by bestselling author Jason R. Rich, visit his Web site at www.JasonRich.com.

202 High-Paying Jobs You Can Land Without a College Degree
Smart Debt

Entrepreneur Magazine's Pocket Guides

Dirty Little Secrets: What the Credit Bureaus Won't Tell You
Why Rent? Own Your Dream Home
Mortgages and Refinancing: Get the Best Rates
Mutual Funds: A Quick-Start Guide
Get that Raise!

Entrepreneur Magazine's Business Traveler Series

Entrepreneur Magazine's Business Traveler Guide to Las Vegas
and coming soon …
Entrepreneur Magazine's Business Traveler Guide to Washington, DC
Entrepreneur Magazine's Business Traveler Guide to New York City
Entrepreneur Magazine's Business Traveler Guide to Orlando
Entrepreneur Magazine's Business Traveler Guide to Chicago
Entrepreneur Magazine's Business Traveler Guide to Los Angeles

Glossary

These are the important terms used throughout this book.

ABS—*See* Anti-Lock Braking System.

Annual percentage rate (APR)—The yearly cost of credit expressed as a percentage; used in finance agreements. In leasing agreements, the equivalent is the *money factor*. All lenders are obligated by law to disclose a loan's APR.

Annual Premium—The total price for insurance coverage for a specified period of time (typically one year). This premium can often be divided into monthly payments to make it more affordable.

AnnualCreditReport.com—A centralized service operated by the three credit reporting agencies (credit bureaus) that processes all requests from consumers who wish to receive their free credit report from each agency.

Anti-Lock Braking System (ABS)—A computer-controlled braking system that monitors the speed of the wheels and senses if braking is causing any difference in wheel speed that indicates a wheel is seizing and, if so, pulses the brakes to prevent that problem so the driver can maintain steering control.

APR—*See* Annual Percentage Rate.

As Is—This means simply that, whatever the condition of the vehicle, the buyer is assuming total responsibility for it and for any repairs. No warranty or guarantee is offered by the seller, whether manufacturer, dealership, or private seller. Vehicles offered "as is" tend to be cheaper, but offer the least peace of mind for the buyer. Another term for "as is" used by dealers is "with all faults." In certain states, if a car is sold "as is," any implied warranties that may otherwise be enforceable do not apply. In other words, you're not protected by any "lemon laws."

Auto Lease Agreement—A legally binding document between a lessor and a lessee that outlines the details, terms, and limitations of the lease, as well as the length, costs, and fees associated with it. Also known as a *lease*.

Automobile Insurance—Insurance that protects against losses involving motor vehicles. The basic types of coverage are bodily injury liability, property damage liability, medical payments or personal injury protection, collision, comprehensive physical damage, and uninsured or underinsured motorist.

Bodily Injury Liability—Insurance coverage that pays your legal defense costs and claims against you or family members living with you and others driving your vehicle with your permission if your vehicle is involved in an accident that causes injury or death.

Capitalized Cost (Cap Cost)—The negotiated total price of a new vehicle being leased. It's comparable to the negotiated price of a new vehicle being purchased.

Certified Pre-owned (CPO)—The current term for "reconditioned and used." Authorized dealerships take their off-lease vehicles—vehicles that have been leased and are usually less than five years old—and put them through an inspection process, attach an extended warranty and other perks, and sell them.

Closed-End Lease—A vehicle lease that ends at the conclusion of the term: the lessee returns the vehicle and has no further responsibilities (other than to pay for any excessive mileage or repair work). In a closed-end lease, the lessor must predict the residual value of the vehicle. This type of lease is generally more suitable for the average person. Closed-end lease payments are somewhat higher than open-end lease payments. Also known as a *walk-away lease*.

Collision—Insurance coverage that pays for damages to your vehicle if your vehicle is involved in a collision with another vehicle or any other object or in a rollover, regardless of who is responsible.

Comprehensive Physical Damage—Insurance coverage that pays for losses if your vehicle suffers damages from theft, fire, hail, wind, flood, vandalism, falling objects, or various other causes (excluding collision or upset).

Convertible—Typically a small car, a convertible has a removable or retractable roof and is more suitable for driving in a warm climate. Most convertibles offer ample seating for two adults. Some offer a small backseat area with limited legroom and stowage space.

CPO—*See* Certified Pre-owned.

Credit Bureau—*See* Credit Reporting Agency.

Credit History—*See* Credit Rating.

Credit Rating—An educated estimate of a person's creditworthiness, a prediction of the likelihood that the person will pay a debt and the extent to which the lender is protected in the event of default.

Credit Report—A credit file disclosure compiled by one of the credit reporting agencies—Equifax, Experian, or TransUnion—that contains personal and financial information about a person, including name, address, phone number, Social Security number, date of birth, past addresses, current and past employers, a listing of companies that have issued credit to that person (including credit cards, charge cards, car loans, mortgages, student loans, and home equity loans), and details about his or her credit history.

Credit Reporting Agency (aka credit bureau)—Any of the three national bureaus—Equifax, Experian, and TransUnion—that maintain credit histories on virtually all Americans with any credit history and supply creditors and lenders with timely and reliable financial reports as requested.

Credit Score—A mathematical calculation of a person's creditworthiness, in which a credit reporting agency applies a complex formula to his or her current financial situation and credit history. A credit score will be between 300 and 850. The national average is about 678. To qualify for a mortgage typically requires a credit score of at least 620.

Dealer Holdback—An allowance that a manufacturer provides to a dealer, usually two to three percent of the MSRP, often as a credit to the dealer's account. With a holdback, the dealer could pay the manufacturer less than the amount invoiced and then sell a vehicle at cost and still make a small profit.

Dealer-Installed Options—Extras that a vehicle buyer selects at the time of purchase and the dealership then professionally installs using genuine products from the vehicle manufacturer. Examples of dealer-installed options include a luggage or bike rack, alloy wheels, floor mats, upgraded stereo systems (including satellite radio), a DVD video system, anti-theft alarm system, fog lights, and a wide range of exterior items to customize the look of the vehicle.

Deductible—The amount the holder of the insurance policy must pay out-of-pocket before the insurance company pays the remainder of a covered loss, up to the specified coverage limits. A deductible can be anywhere from zero to $1,500 or higher. The lower the deductible, the higher the annual premium.

Demonstrator—A vehicle that has never been owned, leased, or used as a rental. It could have been used for test-drives and/or driven by the dealer's staff. It has very low mileage and the full manufacturer's warranty, is typically in like-new condition, and can be purchased for a little less than a new vehicle.

Depreciation—The loss of value of a vehicle over a given time. What it is worth at any given time is the *residual value*.

Disposition Fee—A fee often charged by a lessor to cover the costs of preparing and selling the lease vehicle at the end of the lease. Also known as a *disposal fee* and a *termination fee*.

EPA—U.S. Environmental Protection Agency, source of mileage estimates of fuel economy.

EPA Size Class—Any of the categories into which the Environmental Protection Agency groups motor vehicles—passenger cars according to interior volume and light trucks according to gross vehicle weight rating, the weight of the vehicle, and its carrying capacity—for comparisons of fuel economy.

FICO® Score—Another term for your credit score. FICO® is a registered trademark of Fair Isaac Corporation (NYSE:FIC), the pioneer of the FICO® credit score that's used by many lenders to evaluate consumer credit risk. Scores calculated by credit reporting agencies from models developed by Fair Isaac Corporation are commonly called FICO® scores. These scores are derived solely from the information available on credit reporting agency reports. For a fee, you can obtain your FICO® score online at *www.myfico.com.*

Fleet Car—A vehicle from a group of vehicles owned by a company and driven by employees. Such a vehicle may have been abused by its drivers and could have a lot of wear. A former rental car would fall into this category.

Four-Door Sedan—A full-size vehicle, with comfortable seating for four to five adults, ample trunk stowage space, and plenty of legroom. These cars are designed for comfort and typically offer a wide range of features, like a high-end sound system, a *g*lobal positioning system (GPS), cruise control, electric windows and locks, power seats, superior climate control, and cup holders.

Fuel Economy—The number of miles a vehicle gets per gallon. All vehicle manufacturers are required to show on the sticker the fuel economy of each model, as estimates from the U.S. Environmental Protection Agency for city driving, highway driving, and combined driving.

Full-Size Car—A car that can seat four or five adults comfortably and has ample trunk stowage space and plenty of legroom. A full-size vehicle is often a top choice as a family vehicle, since it also has many safety features. This is often a four-door sedan.

Gap Insurance—A policy on a leased vehicle that covers the policyholder's termination liability under the lease contract if the vehicle is deemed a complete loss before the end of the lease term. It covers the difference between what the lessee owes and the value of the vehicle at the time of the loss. Gap insurance is typically associated with vehicles that are totaled or stolen. Also known as *gap coverage* or *gap protection*.

Gas Mileage—*See* Fuel Economy.

Global Positioning System (GPS)—A system that uses satellite signals to determine the location of a radio receiver, such as mounted in a vehicle.

HEV—Hybrid Vehicle.

Holdback—*See* Dealer Holdback.

Hybrid Electric Vehicle (HEV)—Any vehicle that uses an electric motor with batteries and a gas- or diesel-powered engine.

Hybrid Vehicle—Any vehicle that uses two or more sources of power, typically an electric motor with batteries and a gas- or diesel-powered engine (hybrid electric vehicle, HEV).

Implied Warranty—An obligation under state laws for dealers to ensure that the vehicles they sell meet reasonable quality standards. In some states, any used vehicle sold by a dealer comes with an implied warranty, whether or not a formal written warranty is provided. However, in most states dealers can use the words "as is" or "with all faults" in a written notice to buyers to eliminate implied warranties. There is no specified time period for implied warranties.

Incentive—Any of several means by which a manufacturer encourages the sales of specific vehicles. It could be a discount offered to a dealership or a cash refund or lower loan rate on a vehicle.

Invoice Price—What a dealer pays a manufacturer for a car, exclusive of holdbacks and other discounts. It's usually not what the vehicle actually costs the dealer.

Kelley Blue Book Value—The market value of a vehicle according to a company that's been the industry expert on used car values for 80 years and the source of prices made available on most Web sites. There are two editions of the printed Blue Book—one for consumers and one for dealers: *Kelley Blue Book Auto Market Report—Official Guide.*

Lease—*See* Auto Lease Agreement and Vehicle Lease.

Lemon Law—A colloquial term for any law that establishes standards of quality and performance for motor vehicles. There is a federal law—the Magnuson-Moss Warranty Act— and every state has a law. The state lemon laws differ from state to state. Not all state laws cover used or leased vehicles.

Lessee—The party that acquires use of a vehicle from a *lessor* through a lease.

Lessor—The company that allows use of a vehicle to a *lessee* through a lease.

Luxury Car—Typically, a full-size, mid- to high-priced vehicle that offers top-of-the-line features and options. Comfort, aesthetics, and luxury are the primary focus of the design. These vehicles tend to be status symbols. A high-end audio system, a GPS, leather seats, a sunroof, separate driver/front passenger climate controls, cup holders that heat or cool beverages, a rearview camera, and real wood trim are among the popular features in many luxury vehicles.

Manufacturer's Suggested Retail Price (MSRP)—The price set by the manufacturer for the vehicle as it comes from the factory. The MSRP is typically *not* the price a consumer pays for the vehicle.

Manufacturer-Installed Options—Extras that the manufacturer installs in a vehicle before shipping it to the dealership. This includes such things as air conditioning, automatic transmission, anti-lock brake systems (ABS), leather seats, power windows, power locks, and exterior/interior color combinations.

Medical Payments or Personal Injury Protection—Insurance coverage that pays medical expenses and possibly other expenses (such as lost earnings, rehabilitation, replacement of services, and funeral expenses, depending on the policy) for you or any passengers in your vehicle if your vehicle is involved in an accident and pays medical expenses and possibly other expenses for you or family members injured or killed while riding in another vehicle or injured by another vehicle while walking.

Mid-Size Car—A vehicle smaller than a full-size sedan, with comfort and features but slightly less stowage space. A typical mid-size car has either two or four doors, can hold four or five passengers, and has a small to mid-size trunk (capable of holding one large or two small suitcases).

Minivan/Cargo Van—A large vehicle, capable of holding seven passengers with plenty of stowage space. Many of these vehicles offer fold-down or removable seats, allowing additional stowage space. Many minivans have three to five doors—two in the front, one or two sliding side doors, and a rear door (offering access to stowage space).

Money Factor—A figure that represents the interest rate charged for a lease, used in calculating the monthly payments. The money factor is the interest rate percentage divided by 2,400. (In this formula, 2,400 is always used, regardless of the length of the loan.) To convert a money factor to an interest rate, APR, multiply by 2,400. Dealers will sometimes quote a money factor as a larger decimal (multiplied by 100). Also called a *lease factor*, a *lease fee*, or simply a *factor*.

Monroney Sticker—The sticker on the window of almost every new vehicle sold in the United States, showing the make, model, year, the base price, the manufacturer's installed options, the manufacturer's suggested retail price, the freight or transportation charge, and the fuel economy (mileage). Nobody but the buyer can legally remove this sticker. It's named for Sen. Almer Monroney, who was the main sponsor of the Automobile Information Disclosure Act of 1958, which mandated this sticker.

Monroney Sticker Price—*See* Manufacturer's Suggested Retail Price.

Motor Vehicle Excise Tax—*See* Vehicle excise tax.

MSRP—*See* Manufacturer's Suggested Retail Price.

National Institute for Automotive Service Excellence (ASE)—A nonprofit organization that offers comprehensive testing and certification of automotive technicians and mechanics, who then have the right to refer to themselves as ASE Certified Technicians and the responsibility to follow a strict code of ethics.

Open-End Lease—A vehicle lease that requires the lessee at the conclusion of the term to pay any difference between the residual value of the vehicle and the market value. An open-end lease allows unlimited mileage. This type of lease is used primarily for commercial purposes; it is typically not suitable for personal use. Also known as a *finance lease*.

Personal Injury Protection—*See* Medical Payments or Personal Injury Protection.

Pick-Up Truck—A vehicle with a front compartment that can hold two to six people (depending on the make and model) and an open cargo box. A pick-up truck is ideal for transporting large and heavy items and for towing. It can be driven on a wide range of terrains and in harsh weather conditions. One aspect to consider with pick-up trucks is payload capacity—how much weight the vehicle can carry.

Price, Invoice—*See* Invoice Price.

Program Car—A vehicle that may be relatively new (less than two or three years old) and have relatively low mileage, but it was used as a short-term lease vehicle or as a rental vehicle, so it may have been driven by many people, who may or may not have maintained it properly.

Property Damage Liability—Insurance coverage that pays your legal defense costs and claims against you or family members living with you and others driving your vehicle with your permission, but not the cost of damages to your property, including your vehicle, if your vehicle damages another's property.

Rebate—The amount by which a manufacturer reduces the price of a vehicle. Typically the buyer can apply a rebate to the price of the vehicle or receive it in cash.

Resale Value—The current value of a used car, based on the year, make, model, mileage, and condition. This value will differ depending on whether the vehicle is being sold by a private seller or being accepted as a trade-in by a dealership. Dealerships buy used vehicles based on their wholesale value.

Residual Value—The worth of a vehicle at a given time, the difference between the purchase price and the amount of *depreciation*. In a vehicle lease, this value is estimated at the beginning of the lease and used as the basis for calculating the monthly payments. The actual value of the vehicle at the end of the lease period could be significantly higher or lower.

Small/Compact Car—Usually a two-door coupe or a three-door hatchback capable of seating two to four adults. These cars tend to offer better gas mileage than mid-to-full-size vehicles, but less stowage space.

Sport Utility Vehicle (SUV)—A mid- to full-size vehicle with plenty of space, seating for five to seven people, and plenty of stowage space. These are a top choice among families, particularly in the suburbs, although their popularity has spread considerably. SUVs offer features designed to provide maximum comfort; of particular interest to families, many SUVs now come with a DVD video system in addition to a full-featured sound system and satellite radio receiver. These vehicles are designed for safety in virtually all weather conditions and typically offer real-time four-wheel drive or constant four-wheel drive. Due to their size and weight, unfortunately SUVs have lower fuel economy.

Sports Car—Typically a small car, a sports car has a sleek, aerodynamic design and is typically designed for performance and speed, although it's often for status as much as for performance. Most sports cars offer ample seating for two adults. Some have a small backseat area with limited legroom and stowage space.

Station Wagon/Five-Door—A car with a passenger compartment that extends to the back, where there is a tailgate or a liftgate. A station wagon was a popular choice for a family car prior to the introduction of the SUV and the minivan. These vehicles tend to be larger and heavier, with more safety features and more stowage space. Many station wagons offer the comfort and features of a luxury sedan, but significantly more passenger and stowage space.

Sticker Price—*See* Manufacturer's Suggested Retail Price.

SUV—*See* Sport Utility Vehicle.

Trade-in Value—The amount a dealership credits a buyer for his or her current vehicle as partial payment for another vehicle. This amount is typically about five percent less than the wholesale market value of the trade-in vehicle.

Two-Door Coupe—A compact vehicle, with two doors and typically comfortable seating for two adults. Some vehicles offer a small backseat, but legroom is often limited. Stowage space is also limited.

Uninsured or Underinsured Motorist—Insurance coverage that pays for any resulting costs if an uninsured, underinsured, or hit-and-run driver causes property damage or injuries to you or family members and other passengers in your vehicle.

Upside-Down—A situation in which the balance outstanding on a vehicle loan is greater than the current value of that vehicle.

Vehicle Excise Tax—A local annual tax based on the value of the vehicle, levied by the city or town where the vehicle is principally garaged. The tax rate and the calculation of the amount vary by region.

Vehicle Identification Number (VIN)—A unique serial number given to every vehicle manufactured and imprinted on the vehicle. The VIN is used to register the vehicle with the state Department of Motor Vehicles or Registry of Motor Vehicles. It can be used to track a vehicle's history.

Vehicle Lease—A legal agreement between the *lessor* and the *lessee* about the use of a vehicle. A lease is documented by a contract that specifies the terms and limitations of that use, the length of the agreement, and the monthly payment for use of that vehicle. A typical vehicle lease can last for 24, 36, 48, or 60 months.

VIN—*See* Vehicle Identification Number.

Walk-away lease—*See* Closed-End Lease.

Warranty—A guarantee, either implied or written, that a vehicle will function and perform as specified. It usually covers specified mechanical problems during a specified period of time or for a specified number of miles.

Index

relation to leasing companies,
125, 135, 142
researching, 171
trustworthiness, 105–106
used vehicle, 121–122
as vehicle information resource,
23
Dealer sticker prices, 88–89
Deductibles
defined, 206
impact on insurance premiums,
213
setting appropriate levels, 209,
219
Delivery charges, 16, 88–89
Demonstrators, 120
Depreciation, 61–62, 125–126
Destination charges, 88–89, 97–98
Discontinued models, 120
Discounts (accessory), 189
Discounts (insurance), 214, 222
Disposition fees, 126
Dodge Web site, 24
Down payments, 28, 52, 131
Dress, judging buyers by, 74, 75
Driver age, impact on insurance
premiums, 213
Driving conditions, as selection fac-
tor, 5–6
Driving experience, as selection fac-
tor, 80
Driving habits
impact on fuel economy, 229,
236–237
as vehicle selection factor, 2, 4–7
Driving records, impact on insur-
ance premiums, 212, 220

Duration of loans, 93–95

E

Early terminations (lease)
fees, 133, 136
as leasing disadvantage, 133,
140–141
transfers, 137–138
Edmunds.com Web site, 22, 157,
226
Edmunds True Market Value, 88,
107, 157
Emotional buying decisions, 59,
168–169, 176
Employment, impact on insurance
premiums, 213
Entertainment systems, 199–200
Environmental impact of hybrids,
227, 229
Equifax, 32, 36, 42
Errors in credit reports, 49
"Excellent condition," defined, 109
Excise taxes, 15, 98
Experian
AutoCheck service, 153
fees, 43
as major credit bureau, 32, 36
Web site, 42
Expert interviews
Berman, Bradley, 234–237
Chee, Brian, 172–179
Cunniff, Chris, 216–223
Hearn, Al, 138–145
Nerad, Jack, 162–171
Perleberg, Mark, 179–186
Extended service contracts, 14
Extended warranties, 14, 63, 64

Buy or Lease a Car Without Getting Taken for a Ride